MW00469823

A WORLD AFTER LIBERALISM

A WORLD AFTER LIBERALISM

Philosophers of the Radical Right

Matthew Rose

Yale
UNIVERSITY PRESS
NEW HAVEN & LONDON

Yale University Press books may be purchased in quantity
for educational, business, or promotional use. For information, please e-mail
sales.press@yale.edu (U.S. office) or sales@yaleup.co.uk (U.K. office).

Designed by Dustin Kilgore.
Set in Yale New and Alternate Gothic types by Integrated Publishing Solutions.
Printed in the United States of America.

Library of Congress Control Number: 2020950579
ISBN 978-0-300-24311-6 (hardcover : alk. paper)

A catalogue record for this book is available from the British Library.

This paper meets the requirements of ANSI/NISO Z39.48-1992
(Permanence of Paper).

10 9 8 7 6 5 4 3 2 1

For Caroline

CONTENTS

ACKNOWLEDGMENTS

This book began as an article published in *First Things* magazine and I am grateful to its extraordinary editors for supporting my writing in its earliest stages. I also wish to thank the Berkeley Institute – no scholar could ask for a more supportive institutional home or for more wonderful colleagues. For help with research, I thank Kate Arenchild, Heather Breaux, and archivists at Yale University and the University of Illinois at Urbana-Champagne. Most of all, I thank my wife, Caroline, for supporting a project that does not exactly lend itself to dinner table discussion with two small children. This book is dedicated to her.

Chapter Five previously appeared as "The Outsider" in *First Things* magazine (October 2019) and reappears here with only minor changes. A few paragraphs in the conclusion have been adapted from writing that appeared in "The Anti-Christian Alt-Right" (*First Things,* March 2018) and "The World Turned Upside Down" (*First Things,* February 2020).

A WORLD AFTER LIBERALISM

Introduction

AFTER LIBERALISM

What comes after liberalism? We know what came before it: oppression, ignorance, violence, and superstition. The myth of our political origins is the story of how we learned to build societies on the values of freedom and equality, rather than the accidents of birth and the cruelties of power. It celebrates our liberation from coercive authority, and the growing awareness of our autonomy. The power of this myth, and even our sincere belief in it, has never stopped us from questioning it. Our culture is filled with stories that imagine a heroic world before the comforts and mediocrity of our own. They imagine the courage and gallantry that it inspired, and prompt us to wonder what has been lost in exchanging its noble codes for greater security. But whether their characters wear swords or Stetsons, these stories tell us that their world will never be, and can never be, ours again. It might have inspired braver men and greater deeds, but there is no going back. The frontier is closed.

To ask what came before liberalism is to leave our world safely intact. To ask what comes after liberalism, however, is to threaten it. It is to ponder what is supposed to be unthinkable, and to anticipate what is supposed to be impossible. It is to assume, if only for a disorienting moment, that the direction of history is fundamentally different than what we have long believed. It is to contemplate the shattering possibility that we have been wrong about what human beings are and what they will become. It is not, to be sure, that we ever assumed the work of politics was concluded. If anything, liberalism roused us from complacency, inspiring us to find injustices still hidden and victims still unrecognized. It told us that people should be free to choose their own paths in life and that government ought to protect the exercise of this freedom. But while carrying out its commission, even amid sharp disagreements, we took its future for granted. We assumed history would celebrate the rightness of its values and the sanctity of its causes. The idea that the future might judge it critically was inconceivable. Or at least it once was.

We are living in a postliberal moment. After three decades of dominance, liberalism is losing its hold on Western minds. Its most serious challenge does not come from regimes in China, Russia, or Central Europe, whose leaders declare the liberal epoch is "at an end."[1] It comes from within Western democracies themselves, where intelligent critics, and not just angry populists, are expressing doubts about its most basic norms. Critiques of liberalism are as old as liberalism itself, of course, and its ideas have never gone unchallenged. For centuries, philosophers have questioned it from all sides. They have blamed it for increasing inequality and exploitation, and for corrupting culture and religion. They have been especially skeptical of its vision of human beings as rights-bearing individuals who are defined by their ability to choose. But if our moment is not novel in every respect, it is jarringly new to some of us. The idea that human equality, minority rights, religious toleration, or cultural pluralism might be rejected out of principle, and not blind prejudice, is bewildering to many. They are ideas associated with antiquated books and defeated causes – with people living in the past, not looking toward the future.

A new conservatism, unlike any in recent memory, is coming into view. Ideas once thought taboo are being reconsidered; authors once banished are being rehabilitated; debates once closed are reopening. There is disagreement about how this intellectual space opened up, but there is no doubt who is filling it. Nationalists, populists, identitarians, futurists, and religious traditionalists are vying to define conservatism in ways previously unimaginable. To a remarkable degree, they dissent from an orthodoxy that seemed settled as recently as 2016. They take as a premise, not a possibility, that American conservatism as it has defined itself for generations is intellectually dead. Its defense of individual liberty, limited government, and free trade is today a symptom of political decadence, they argue, not its solution. Perhaps more significant, they see it as an obstacle to the future they already embody: a political right prepared to dismantle liberal institutions, not simply manage their decline.

Young, countercultural, and dismissive of conventional opinion, these conservatives have fomented debates that will seem esoteric to outsiders. They range from a recovery of ancient paganism to defenses of the medieval papacy. They promote theories of elite dominance and rules for grassroots radicals. They imagine futures in outer space and on farms. They envision new industrial policies and new liberal arts colleges. Their debates feature atheists and Catholics, racists and minorities, coders and agrarians. If this postliberal landscape sounds bizarre, you are not alone. Its arguments are rarely discussed in mainstream publications, and certainly not in the legacy media.[2] They are found in self-published books, pseudonymous podcasts, and short-lived websites, all publicized through anonymous social media accounts. They have raised up new luminaries in place of old ones. Instead of William Buckley it is Curtis Yarvin. Instead of Milton Friedman it is Peter Thiel. Instead of George Will it is Angelo Codevilla. Instead of Richard John Neuhaus it is Adrian Vermeule. Instead of Irving Kristol it is Steve Sailer. That you might be unfamiliar with some of these names does not make you unusual. In congressional offices, Republican politicians won't know them all either, but their young aides will. At conservative magazines, senior editors don't read them, but their junior staff do.

On what do the postliberals agree? On almost nothing. They disagree profoundly on race, religion, economics, and political strategy. Some focus obsessively on immigration and demographic change, others on economic stagnation or the collapse of religious authority. But they all agree on this: new forms of political life will soon be possible. If they are hopeful about a prospect that others fear, it is because they foresee a revolution in conservative thinking. National solidarity and cultural identity, not individual liberty, will be its principal themes – a conservatism focused on public goods, not private interests. In charting this path, the postliberal right takes inspiration from the progressive left. The left, it concedes, got something right. It understood that for political change to be possible, it must first be *conceivable*. Feminism, marriage equality, racial justice, multiculturalism – the left governed political life by controlling how we imagined the arc of history. It convinced Americans that history progressed by removing barriers to inclusion and equality, assumptions that left conservatives with little to say about the destination of our culture, only the speed at which we arrived. For the postliberals, we are nearing a time when these roles might be reversed.

If the new right has claimed the future, it is largely powerless at present. It has no political representation, no policy platform, and no institutional base. To espouse the views of integralism, neoreaction, or the alt-right, as some of its most radical factions are called, is to commit professional suicide. But appearances can be deceptive, and politics is a lagging indicator of cultural change. Listen closely, read carefully, and ignore the noise of social media, and you will detect a generational shift on the intellectual right. Young conservatives are seeking a new theoretical basis for our politics, a conceptual framework that makes sense of the failures of the right and the successes of the left. They are second-guessing older arguments in their movement's canon, especially those placing individual liberty above the common good. They are instead looking furtively to dissident authors and taboo traditions, contemplating the cultural, spiritual, and even racial foundations of human identity.[3]

There is no knowing for certain what this postliberal mood portends. No synthesis of its factions is possible, and it is foolish to make predictions about elections. But history offers a guide to the destiny of ideas, and we would be wise to follow it where we can. This is not a book about a present generation of radicals, but about a previous one, who also sought to break through the mental prison of liberalism and to build societies on truths that had been hidden or suppressed. It offers a general introduction to one of the most controversial bodies of political thought in the twentieth century. The radical right, as I call them, anticipated the end of liberalism and the dawn of a postliberal era. Its theories of cultural differences, human inequality, religious authority, and racial biopolitics were widely viewed as invitations to xenophobia and even violence. But whatever their failings, they attempted, as few others have, to imagine a world after centuries of liberal dominance. I do not claim we are fated to repeat their arguments, and certainly not to admire their character. But they can serve as guides to some of the lurking political possibilities of our time, helping us to better understand what some radicals have already discovered, and what more will likely find.

Conservative Revolutions

What would a postliberal right look like? One answer to this question can be found in a body of thought that developed in response to the Second World War. I call these thinkers the radical right, though not because they represent the most extreme expression of right-wing opinion. They are radical in the double sense of seeking a fundamentally new basis for conservative thought, and in the revolutionary consequences they draw from it. On both points they offered different and frequently conflicting visions. They advanced cultural, spiritual, and materialist theories of political life, from which they imagined revolutions from above and below, and led by the few and the many. They offered interpretations of art and religion, as well as examinations of class conflict and corporate governance. Their writings sometimes influenced political power at the highest levels, and other times languished in mimeographed obscurity. But despite differences in substance and style, these thinkers nurtured an intellectual community, existing on the far margins of every Western nation, that came to see itself as a distinct philosophical tradition.

It claimed its intellectual roots in a previous generation of "new conservatives" that emerged in Germany after 1918. They are collectively known as the "Conservative Revolution," an oxymoronic term suggesting their ambition to synthesize traditional and modernist thinking. Its chief figures included Carl Schmitt, Ernst Jünger, Arthur Moeller van den Bruck, and Oswald Spengler. Most of its members rejected the Nazi regime and its racial doctrines, some at significant personal cost. But they also sought a path for the West beyond the twin evils of Anglo-American liberalism and Soviet communism, whose ideals they blamed for the political chaos and cultural decadence of the Weimar Republic. They argued that human life had been debased by political ideologies that aimed at nothing higher than the peaceful resolution of conflict and the efficient management of consumption. Liberalism had drained politics of meaning, they argued, and its appeals to justice and equality could not summon real human loyalties or inspire true human greatness. But if these thinkers were disgusted by modern culture, they did not believe a return to the prewar status quo was possible or desirable.

The Conservative Revolution sought a conceptual framework that accepted many of the assumptions of modern thought but rejected its conventional political implications. If human reason is unable to know universal truths or absolute moral values, they argued, authority and myth are even more important in politics; if the pursuit of power is a basic drive of human nature, a pacified world is not a human world. They therefore envisioned a conservatism that emphasized the irrational aspects of human nature, celebrating our need for risk and danger. They also stressed the need for a ruling elite that could inspire the masses to pursue values beyond individual happiness. What was striking about these views, and what distinguished them from the clerical and monarchist right, was that they did not seek to reverse the process of modernization. They sought to accelerate it, believing that new political possibilities, previously hidden or forbidden, would be revealed in its development.

For some, this included a critical reassessment of the place of Christianity in Western culture. They wondered if Christian moral teachings, long assumed to be a source of moral order, might actually be a source of social decadence.[4]

The Conservative Revolution essentially dissolved after 1933, when some of its members went into internal emigration and others met early deaths. Today the movement is remembered chiefly for its gloomy brand of *Kulturkritik* and attacks on parliamentary democracy that cleared the way for a tyranny that many of them despised. Its thinkers never agreed on a political ideology, but its ideas, as well as its heterodox attitude, helped to inspire a new form of radical conservatism. Its features, as we will see, at first appeared to be a simple and even simplistic inversion of classical liberalism. It saw humans as naturally tribal, not autonomous; individuals as inherently unequal, not equal; politics as grounded in authority, not consent; societies as properly closed, not open; and history as cyclical, not progressive. Each of these ideas had roots in European thought, stretching from antiquity to the nineteenth century, and could make no claim to originality. But they were put to novel use in an apocalyptic interpretation of modern civilization.

As it observed Western nations in the postwar era, the radical right did not see growing peace and prosperity as a validation of the liberal principles that informed them. It saw a culture traumatized by its past and terrified of the burdens of political responsibility. It saw a culture appealing to universal principles out of a loss of confidence in own traditions. And it saw a culture blind to the real diversity of peoples and in craven denial of its own differences with them. How had a culture, nearing the height of its global power, lost its own sense of identity? Why had it staked its legitimacy on values that outsiders and enemies could turn against it? The radical right argued that the material strength of Western democracies hid debilitating philosophical and religious weaknesses. Their worry was not that these weaknesses left the West vulnerable to the spread of global communism (the radical right, in fact, often contemplated future alliances with Russia). They feared the West was trapped in a civilizational crisis, amounting to a kind of death wish, that it perversely forbade anybody to identify, let alone attempt to solve.

To explain this pathology, the radical right told a story about liberalism. It argued that as an empirical description of human life, liberalism was demonstrably false. Liberalism imagined that human beings are fundamentally *individuals* who share the same needs and motivations, and whose societies can be peacefully harmonized. But the truth, the radical right countered, is that we inherit ways of thinking and acting that reflect our particular ethno-cultural origins. These origins bind us not only to social groups and to unchosen obligations. They also permanently dispose us to living in a certain way—they incline cultures to different conceptions of art and politics, they incline individuals to different stations in life, and they incline societies to distinguish insiders from outsiders. Our ethno-cultural origins can be denied or suppressed, they can be spiritually ennobled or morally corrupted, but they cannot ultimately be overcome, and it is dangerous to believe they can. It is part of the suicidal nature of liberalism, the radical right claimed, that it represses these primordial facts, empowering groups who do not believe its fictions, and impairing those who do.

But to this empirical critique, the radical right added another. It held that as a moral vision of life, liberalism was evil. Not only in practice, where its understanding of human nature encouraged hedonism, selfishness, and mediocrity. Liberalism is evil in principle because it destroys the foundations of social order. It obscures the central moral distinction, which is not between right and wrong, but between civilization and barbarism. The thinkers of the radical right, as we will see, had different visions of political life. But they agreed that it stands on enforced judgments concerning what is higher and lower, excellent and base, friend and enemy. Politics is properly illiberal about everything, depending, from its smallest decisions to its highest goals, on judgments about human greatness. Liberalism, for its part, promotes the equality of lifestyles, declining to tell citizens how to become virtuous or great. And as a result, it slowly renders people incapable of answering life's most basic question.

Liberalism aimed to free people to discover and express their individual identities, apart from coercive interference. But by uprooting people from historic communities and social roles, the radical right predicted, liberalism would trigger an anxious preoccupation with group belonging. The triumph of liberalism would therefore coincide with its collapse. By pressing people to ask, "Who am I?" its social logic would lead them back to the most basic human question, "Who are we?" At its heart, the radical right was a response to this spiraling crisis of belonging. It argued the crisis could not be solved by returning to conventional national or religious identities, since that would merely restore a sick patient to a condition when its symptoms first appeared. The solution to the crisis would require Western culture to unlearn a millennia-long mistake, sustained by centuries of Christian belief, that attempted to ground its legitimacy outside of itself. Political life does not depend on truths or values that transcend our identities, the radical right claimed, or on a biblical vision of human unity. It depends on recognizing that human identity, at its most primordial level, is something inherited. To an age of growing individualism, this movement's message was powerfully dissonant: Your identity does not belong to you alone. It joins you forever to those of your kind, and separates you forever from those who are alien. To know and to affirm this inheritance is to live a meaningful life; to deny it is the greatest tragedy; to be denied it the greatest injustice.

An Alternative History of the Twentieth Century

This book profiles major intellectual figures of the radical right, accompanying their arguments as they develop across different decades and in different national contexts. It is not a social history. It offers essay-portraits that focus on the arguments and intellectual backgrounds of their subjects. I chose these five thinkers not only because of their central importance and for the fascination they continue to hold for new readers. They each represent an important style of thought, giving expression to one of the major strands of their intellectual tradition. The radical right is not intellectually homogenous. It has several faces, and I aim to sketch their aspects and to capture their family resemblances. I sometimes draw connections between each thinker and political movements, both past and present, but a different book would chronicle their social influence, as well as their intellectual roots, more extensively. My primary goal is to render their ideas intelligible, not to map their legacies.

I begin with Oswald Spengler, the intellectual godfather of the radical right. Today the media has been surprised to discover the role a German historian is playing in guiding the "new right," but they should not be.[5] Spengler has been the inspiration of radical conservatism for a century. His writings anticipated the major fault lines of politics in the third millennium. He foresaw an age of identity politics, in which people increasingly compete for the recognition of their group differences, rather than their individual similarities. He also predicted the role that mass immigration and technology transfer would play in global political realignments. But for all his political prescience, Spengler was essentially a cultural psychologist. He contemplated what a "whiteshift" would mean for the self-image of Europeans and white Americans.[6] How would they react to the demographic and economic rise of the nonwhite world? Spengler believed the West was unprepared for this existential challenge and the civilizational conflicts it portended. His response was to provide Western peoples with what he believed they most desperately needed: a clear understanding of their own identity and its irreconcilable differences with all others.

I next turn to Julius Evola, sometimes called the "Italian Spengler," whose collaboration with fascist movements made him one of continent's most controversial intellectuals in the postwar era. His extraordinary publishing career, stretching over half a century, give him the richest body of work on what he termed the "real right." For two generations of students who visited his Rome apartment, Evola was revered as a kind of spiritual *ronin,* a master whose wartime experiences and intellectual gifts gave him an unrivaled stature. His books sought to revive the assumption of natural human inequality as essential to any political order. He did so through a form of mythic thinking that collapsed the distance between the archaic past and present. Through esoteric readings of ancient and modern texts, he claimed to reveal the permanent constitution of human society, which he envisioned as a form of sacred hierarchy led by an elite order of men. We often associate utopian thinking with the political left. But Evola is without question the most interesting utopian thinker on the right, and he invites us to envision a postliberal world in fantastic, if terrifying, detail.

Francis Parker Yockey is the first of two Americans that I profile. He is the least-known subject of this book, as well as the most difficult to write about with any intellectual charity. Yockey was a fascist savant whose writings in the 1950s aimed at the fundamental orientation of the American far right. His writings were vaulted to lasting notoriety after his high-profile trial and suicide in a San Francisco jail cell in 1960. Yockey lived a life of daring fidelity to his ideals, spending almost a decade traveling under false papers throughout the fascist underground. His activism would have inspired a movie, were it not for the causes that he served. Yockey was America's preeminent theorist of authoritarianism, and one of the first to envision future alliances between a postliberal West and a post-Soviet Russia. His two-volume work *Imperium* set out to reveal the "inner enemies" of Western culture. Yockey's nightmare was not that Jews had taken control of political and economic institutions. It was that Americans, under the influence of "cultural Marxism," were in the process of becoming Jews by adopting their habits of critical reasoning.

No contemporary European thinker has been more influential on the postliberal right than Alain de Benoist, the primary inspiration behind "identitarianism." Benoist's ideas resist simple categories. They took shape in his peculiar response to the intellectual atmosphere of 1968 Paris. As a young activist on the campus far right, Benoist had been influenced by Evola and Yockey, but he saw tantalizing possibilities in the ideas of the New Left: its concern to protect minorities, indigenous peoples, regional cultures, and non-Christian religions. Benoist came to see such ideas as the foundation of a French new right. His theory of "folk democracy" defends the right of all peoples to protect their customs, cultures, and even ethnic integrity from the effects of liberalism. Benoist is a pagan, and his rejection of liberalism flows from his rejection of Christianity, which he, like other thinkers in this book, blames for severing the organic roots of European peoples. Benoist's radical conservatism is not based in claims to Western supremacy, but in its opposite – in a protest against all forms of spiritual conquest and ideological colonization.

I return to the American scene with an examination of the most prescient theorist of Trumpism, Samuel Francis. A columnist and essayist, Francis spent his Beltway career attacking a conservative movement that he believed no longer represented the class interests of its voters. He claimed that Reagan-era conservatism was a glass bead game, its ideas and debates having become a form of intellectual leisure for a protected political class that was blind to the realities of power politics. A right-wing Marxist, he sought to formulate a political doctrine, responsive to the material structures of American life, that could dismantle managerial liberalism. His attempt to foment a "Middle American Revolution" was made in both populist and racial terms, and specifically targeted underclass voters. It synthesized nationalist populism with brewing racial resentments over the shrinking demographic majority of white Americans. If America was to survive as a country, Francis warned, whites would have to learn to identity their interests, as well as their enemies, in explicitly racial terms.

In a final chapter on the "Christian Question" I shift focus and tone, taking up a theological theme that runs quietly throughout the book. It is impossible to study the radical right without noticing its profound suspicion of Christianity, which it identified as the original source (and continuing inspiration) of liberal values. In this respect, it diverged fundamentally from a postwar conservatism that saw Western civilization as dependent on Christian inspiration, as well as from an older tradition of Catholic anti-liberalism, whose very different ideas I hope to examine in a future work. Its point of view will at first seem strange, since it names Christianity as the *cause* of modern values that Christianity is often accused of impeding or rejecting. The radical right critiques Christianity not for restricting individual autonomy, but for inventing it; not for reinforcing human inequalities, but for dismantling them; not for intolerance of outsiders, but for openness to them. We tend to think of anti-Christian arguments as a feature of the secular left, but the oldest criticisms of Christianity, as we will see, actually come from the radical right, who fear that Christianity severs human roots in history and nature. This concluding chapter opens with a discussion of the rise of the alt-right, and then explains in detail why the radical right blamed Christianity for revolutionizing Western culture through its vision of human identity. The ideas of the radical right invite serious responses from a range of secular and religious traditions, which can each bring to bear important insights of their own; if this book succeeds in eliciting them, I would be enormously pleased. For my part, I close the book in a Christian voice, reflecting on the idea that Christian faith, rather than uprooting believers from their communal pasts, restores their true ancestors and homeland.

Sine Ira et Studio

To write "without anger or zeal" was the aim of ancient historians trying to understand the recent past, worried that their personal passions might cloud their vision. I have been guided by this ideal throughout a study of materials that I sometimes found loathsome and pseudo-academic. But one cannot write out of disgust—or at least one cannot write well—and I have labored to show that these authors also offer moments of real insight and reward careful study. There is no denying that some of their ideas offend popular notions of justice and decency, and no disputing that they reflect some of the most troubling aspects of our humanity. I hope that in treating them seriously I have done nothing to normalize any of the perennial diseases of the human mind.

But for just these reasons, and for just those worries, I believe this work is important. Our political culture, on both the left and right, has narrowed to a suffocating degree. The same slogans, clichés, and euphemisms impose themselves on our minds inflexibly, restricting the range of thought and expression that our society needs. We are too often denied, and we too often deny to others, the freedom to entertain radically alternative views of what it means to be a human being. But no human values can be sustained by intimidation and shaming, and no liberalism worth saving can be practiced, let alone defended, in an atmosphere of ideological bullying. If it is paramount that we judge these thinkers critically, it is also paramount that we find them comprehensible. We cannot judge what we do not understand, and we cannot know where we ought to go without knowing what other possibilities exist.

The radical right is the true "other" in our culture. Unlike the radical left, its authors are not found in university curricula, and sometimes not even in university libraries. Nor are its ideas and believers thoughtfully depicted in our literature, entertainment, or art.[7] We know them as moral monsters, as cynical exploiters of hatred, or as ignorant of the education and experience that disprove their errors. We picture them in cabins in Idaho broadcasting over shortwave radio, not as scholars or artists who can read Sanskrit. And who can deny that we have reasons for imagining them so? What we find the most difficult to understand, however, is what I came to realize is the most essential to appreciate. I speak of the moral quality of their protest. For the thinkers in this book do not believe they are nihilists, as we might believe, but the last remaining enemies of nihilism on this side of the liberal frontier. Our word for this is idealist. Their ideals are not mine and are likely not yours, but their writings tell us they are engaged in a lonely struggle to save wisdom and civilization from those who would see them destroyed. Their cause assumes that an open society is incompatible with the demands of civilized life. For us to dispel the closed society they dream of, we must begin by understanding it.[8]

Chapter 1

THE PROPHET

Oswald Spengler thought he could see into the future, but in the summer of 1933, he seemed blind to the present. Nazi censors had not yet suppressed his new book, *The Hour of Decision*, and the reprieve, he knew, would be temporary. Spengler had rushed the book into print before being finished (it still bears the subtitle "Part One") and he was careful to make no direct mention of national socialism or of Hitler, who had risen to power just months before its publication. The book made clear Spengler's decision that Hitler was not the leader that he, like others on the revolutionary right, had hoped for. While he admitted that he welcomed the collapse of the Weimar Republic, his attacks on its successor regime, however veiled, meant he would never be permitted to publish in Germany again.

Although the book sold well, Spengler's view of world politics perplexed readers looking for an analysis of developments in his native country. If the hour of decision was nearing, he had unusual ideas as to what the decision was about. One thing was confusingly clear: it was not primarily about Hitler, whom Spengler wrote off as insignificant after a private meeting, their first and only, shortly before the book's release.[1] *The Hour of Decision* insinuated that Hitler was an "idiot" and did little to conceal Spengler's contempt for a movement filled with the "dregs" of society and motivated by "nihilism" and "hatred." Yet the ideological debates that had roiled the interwar years did not impress its author either, and Spengler dismissed the coming world war as a mere ripple in the deep flow of time. "I write not for a few months ahead or for the next year, but for the future," he announced. "I see further than others. I see not only great possibilities, but also great dangers."[2]

Spengler had made his name as a prophet of cultural decline, and his final prediction was his most provocative. He predicted a crisis, the "most severe" in human history, that would test the strength of the entire Western world. At present "no one sees, or dares to see it," but the willingness of Europeans and Americans to face it together, without the false comfort of illusions or sentimentality, would determine the shape of history.[3] What did Spengler see? Near the turn of the millennium, the West would confront the "colored world-revolution," the rise of "colored" nations into positions of increasing parity with the "white world." The revolution will not arrive by force of arms, he cautioned. It will arrive as Asian, African, Latin American, and Middle Eastern peoples, equipped with Western science and technology, realize that the era of global white supremacy is over. Having at last "come to feel their own common strength," they will set out to enter modernity on their own terms, without colonial supervision. *This* revolution, and not the one underway in Germany, will present the true hour of decision.[4]

Spengler attempted to distinguish his views, and his fears, from the racist doctrines that would soon inspire a human catastrophe. He pleaded that, unlike the anti-Semites he loathed, he was not concerned with preserving racial purity, and he conceded that centuries of "exploitation" and "grotesque" treatment by whites would lend the revolution moral legitimacy. But Spengler was no humanitarian, and certainly no liberal, and his concern was with the fragile soul of the white world. What will happen to *it*, he wondered, when the "downtrodden races of the outer ring" begin to move from the periphery to the center? What will happen after having shared its technology in an absent-minded act of goodwill? Spengler feared an outcome more deadly than military defeat, economic loss, or demographic decline; he feared a fatal crisis of identity. The developing world lacked comparable economic and military power, but it possessed something more powerful: a firm sense of collective identity and the resolve to preserve it in the third millennium. And its assertive solidarities, Spengler worried, will press a self-doubting and morally sensitive Western world into forsaking its own identity and common interests.[5]

The Hour of Decision is not celebrated as a classic of anti-Nazi literature. Its fear of imagined minorities more than existing fascists seems obtuse, even when allowing for its year of publication. But it is here, at its most fevered and panicked, that Spengler's book feels uncannily prescient. While Spengler did not have a name for what he anticipated, we do: identity politics. He was a prophet, at least in one irrefutable respect. The politics of the third millennium, he predicted, would not replay the intellectual battles of the twentieth century. They would feature the struggle for recognition between diverse human identities and the cultural symbols that reflect them. Spengler wrote to participate in this coming politics, to intensify rather than mitigate a conflict that he believed was inevitable after the demise of liberalism. And his message, encoded in an exhilarating work of speculative history, would become an explosive idea for an intellectual movement he would not live to see. To survive as a people and a culture, Europeans would need to know what set them apart – and Spengler claimed that he alone could tell them.

The Decline of the West

When Spengler retired from teaching in 1910 at the age of thirty, he had grand aspirations, and none of them involved writing one of the most controversial books of the century. He had recently received a small inheritance that allowed him to pursue the intellectual life that had been denied him after failing his doctoral examinations seven years earlier. His studies were in mathematics and the sciences, but his aim was to become a man of letters. Little remains of his early poems, short stories, and librettos, however, and nothing of a planned novel that was to be his masterwork. His ambitions changed abruptly when he glimpsed Otto Seeck's *History of the Decline of the Ancient World* in a Munich bookshop window. A decade-long project flashed before his mind's eye.[6]

The appearance of the first volume of *The Decline of the West* in 1918 transformed an unknown independent scholar into an intellectual celebrity almost overnight. The book was spectacularly, if also inadvertently, well timed. Spengler never intended it as an explanation of Germany's defeat in the war; a nationalist, he had written the book in anticipation of a German victory. Yet its story of the present decay and certain death of European culture, however misunderstood, enabled German readers to make sense of the war and to console themselves with the belief that the same ultimate fate awaited its victors. The book dominated intellectual discussion in what became known as the "Year of Spengler," but its author quickly set to work correcting its popular reception. From the start, he protested that his book was a call to action, not an endorsement of fatalism. "I am not a pessimist," he declared in 1921, shortly before completing its second volume. "Pessimism means not to see any more tasks. I see so many unsolved tasks that I fear we shall have neither time nor men enough to go at them."[7]

The Decline of the West was difficult to categorize and nearly impossible to judge critically. Thomas Mann read it as a novel, Martin Heidegger dismissed it as philosophy, and Northrop Frye praised it as a poem.[8] It adhered to no rules of academic or literary convention, bending and blending genres in a highly personal and kaleidoscopic style. It was a work of poetry that invited theoretical debate, a work of philosophy expressed in images, and a work of history that aimed at spiritual conversion. It offered a sprawling interpretation of world cultures, whose rise and fall formed the dramatic action of human history. Spengler counted eight of them: Western, Classical, Arabian, Indian, Babylonian, Chinese, Egyptian, and Mexican.[9] *Decline* was a monument of humanistic learning, but the study would be almost impossible for any author to complete. Spengler devoted significant attention only to Western, Classical, and Arabian cultures, to which he gave the names Faustian, Apollonian, and Magian. In the work's second volume, he explained that its thin treatment of other cultures was due to a dearth of scholarship. For the most part, scholars were unforgiving and *Decline* died the academic death of a thousand cuts by historians disputing its imaginative reconstructions.

Spengler never claimed to be a historian, however, merely one who had discovered history's meaning and destiny. His was a book "for the benefit of serious readers who are seeking a glimpse of life," not a work of disinterested scholarship.[10] Spengler stood near the end of a German philosophical tradition that sought to explain the mystery of time by showing how its events formed an intelligible process. His approach was innovative, however, and rejected both Christian and Enlightenment views of historical development, as well as the progressive optimism they have sometimes encouraged. History does not have a single direction or destination, Spengler argued. Augustine's belief that it ends in the City of God was no more or less mistaken than Marx's belief that it culminates in communist utopia. There is no plan, no progress, and no personal deity at work in time's unfolding.[11] But neither is history an unintelligible chaos of cause and effect. There is a metaphysical pattern to human life, and if we can learn to perceive its symbolic order, Spengler claimed, we can understand more than past and future shapes of history. We can also know who we are and how we must live.

Cultures and Humanities

The key to human history is found in the diversity of cultures, and the peoples they reflect. Spengler arrived at this position, and its radical political implications, by a cunning route – not by defending a hierarchy of cultures, but by demolishing the very idea. Spengler was both a conservative and a multiculturalist, a synthesis whose dangerous potencies would become attractive to later readers. He began by dismissing any attempt to understand human life from a universal point of view. In an early chapter of *The Decline of the West*, he argued that human beings exist in both nature and history, but in fundamentally different ways. In the realm of nature, we exist as a "zoological" phenomenon that can be studied by the methods of modern science. But the perspective of science, and the academic disciplines that imitate its methods, tell us nothing about our inner identities, Spengler maintained, because as *human* beings we do not exist in a physical universe at all. We live in another, higher dimension of reality, the realm of culture.

The human world is the world of culture. Its universe – our "microcosm," as he suggestively put it – is not defined by the laws of biology and chemistry. It is defined by language, art, music, narrative, ritual, and religion. Like other conservative thinkers of his time, Spengler sought to defend local customs and folk traditions as sources of perennial wisdom. But his understanding of culture, and how it shaped human identities, went beyond romantic traditionalism. He argued that there is no place outside of a particular culture from which human beings can think, feel, or communicate. To participate in a culture is not simply to understand its rules and mores, and it involves more than learning its history, mastering its language, and adopting its values. For Spengler, cultures were perceptual frameworks for understanding and interacting with the world. Languages, rituals, histories, myth, works of art and music – they are the human mode for experiencing reality. They are not just what we know, in other words, they are that *by which* we know. Spengler meant, as some philosophers argue today, that human thought and expression are always a social activity. But he also meant that at one level we do not live in immediate contact with reality – that we do not, indeed cannot, experience a world of brute facts or animal needs and desires. Through culture, we partially transcend nature, and our ability to do so is the distinguishing mark of humanity.[12]

Spengler therefore saw the world as divided into different cultures, whose identities he interpreted in morphological terms. Cultures are like organisms: they live through a cycle of birth, growth, maturity, and death. Spengler is perhaps best known for applying to history the biological concept of living forms. It is an idea that he borrowed from Goethe's philosophy of nature but put to original purposes. Since cultures are a product of human artifice, he reasoned, their histories have the shape of a human life. "Every culture passes through the age-phases of the individual man," he explained. "Each has its childhood, youth, manhood and old age." Although a culture is not a person, it possesses a personality, a unique identity and style. During its lifespan, it gives expression to the animating "form" in which it was originally conceived. How this form comes into existence Spengler failed to say – cultures emerge with seemingly miraculous spontaneity – but it contains, like a seed, all the potentialities, all the possibilities of creative self-expression, that will arise, ripen, and decay in its mortal history.[13]

The Decline of the West offered daring, and occasionally outrageous, interpretations of human cultures and their plurality of forms. Their meanings came into view through what Spengler called their "prime symbol," a notion that is both the least persuasive and most enchanting aspect of the work. Spengler did not just essentialize people – he *destined* them, denying that identity could ultimately ever be a matter of individual choice.[14] He called his method a "universal symbolism." It imagined that cultures are organized around a central symbol, which functions as something like a metaphysical archetype that unconsciously governs the mentality and practices of its members. There are no accidents in a culture, no real diversity, and no profound disagreements. Everything it creates – from its religion and arts to its political institutions and style of warfare – reflects its prime symbol and can be fully understood only in relation to it. Spengler had no scholarly training in non-Western cultures, and *Decline* was audaciously speculative in its approach to history, anthropology, and sociology. But its interpretations of cultural objects, and their symbolic meanings, have captivated readers for over a century.

Spengler structured his book around its disclosures of various symbols. They were revealed through inventive and often beautiful descriptions of cultural artifacts, drawn largely from music and architecture, that attempt to elicit the kind of aesthetic intuition that alone discloses the symbolic configuration of a culture. (To grasp a symbol, Spengler explained, one needs the eye of an artist.[15]) For the Chinese, who "wander" through the natural world, it is the symbol of the garden that illuminates a culture's painting, poetry, and crafts. For the Egyptian, who sees life as a brief passage between past and future life, it is the image of the "narrow path" that structures its visual and liturgical arts. For the Magian culture of the Middle East, home of biblical monotheism, a "cavern" symbolizes its dualistic vision of the cosmos, and guides the development of arabesque, geometry, and its highest architectural expression, the mosque. A Doric column is the archetype of Greek and Roman antiquity, which conceived of perfection in terms of immunity to time. As for the Faustian culture of Europe and America, Spengler envisioned its prime symbol as "infinity," a view, as we will see, that expresses its drive for knowledge and self-mastery.

Human beings can therefore transcend nature, but they cannot transcend their culture and its symbolic horizons. A European cannot really know what it is like to be Chinese, nor can a Mexican truly understand the culture of ancient Rome or Babylon. Cultures are self-contained metaphysical worlds, and the notion of a "multicultural" society is a chimera – all societies are symbolically closed.[16] Spengler acknowledged that individuals engage in the examination and comparison of cultures from within the perspective of their own (his work was one such effort, with all the epistemic limitations it implied). But he maintained that, in a deep sense, cultures are inaccessible and incomprehensible to outsiders who do not inhabit their microcosms of meaning and reference. Spengler did not deny that a set of characteristics is universally shared by members of our species. Yet because human faculties are underdetermined by our biological nature, he argued, they develop only through a culture rooted in a particular history, geography, and even climate. And as these cultures are incommensurably different, so too are human beings.[17]

Spengler was therefore a cultural relativist. Cultures not only have their own psychologies; they possess their own sciences, arts, and politics as well. "There is not one sculpture, one painting, one mathematics, one physics, but many, each in its deepest essence different from the others."[18] Spengler's interpretations were dubious in obvious respects. He forced cultures (and peoples) into preestablished identities, eliminating the diversities and disagreements within them. He was serenely untroubled by the fact that few people had any conscious knowledge of their prime symbols. In other respects, however, he was ahead of his time. *The Decline of the West* opened with an attack, controversial in its day but conventional in ours, on two forms of historiography – one that recognized the nation as the basic unit of historical analysis, and another that placed Europe at the center of world history. His "Copernican" revolution in history rejected every attempt to evaluate non-Western cultures by European standards. "Each culture possesses its own standards, the validity of which begins and ends with it," he declared.[19] For Spengler, the great philosophers of history were therefore all wrong, and so were the Christian theologians, whose legacy he would later criticize bitterly. History does not write with capital letters – no culture is universal, no nation is superior, and no people are chosen. Yet one culture has become uniquely *aware* of its place in history, and its members have a special destiny and face a special danger.

Faustian Man and the Uniqueness of the West

All cultures are unique, but one is more unique than others. "We men of the Western culture," Spengler claimed, "are an exception."[20] At the heart of *The Decline of the West* was an interpretation of the culture he named "Faustian," a term widely used in the intellectual circles of the radical right. As he guided readers through its birth and development, Spengler's intentions became clear. His deepest purpose was not to admire Western culture's past or lament its present. The book was neither an exercise in nostalgia, nor an invitation to stoic acceptance. Spengler's purpose was meta-political. It was to summon readers to recognition of their true identity and to willing acceptance of their culture's revolutionary destiny. To read the book rightly as a (white) European was to realize that one is part of a culture to which one belongs exclusively *and* which belongs exclusively to them. Spengler's relativism took a strategic turn, subversive in its logic, shrewd in its execution, and powerful in its ideological effect. He did not argue, nor did he profess to believe, that the "white world" was superior. He advanced a stronger argument, or so he judged. He argued that European peoples and their culture are *one,* and that any attempt to compromise their unity would be fatal to both.

As with other cultures, a single idea permeates the arts and sciences of the West. According to Spengler, its distinctive mark is an intense striving for "infinity." Under its influence, the West developed into an exceptionally dynamic culture, whose expressions are displayed across its landscape. The glass of Sainte-Chapelle, the harmonies of Corelli, the disputations of Aquinas, the soliloquies of Hamlet, the mathematics of Newton, the fantasies of Don Quixote, the perspective of Rembrandt—Spengler detected everywhere the

Faustian drive toward the infinite. His symbol aimed to capture, in a single archetype, the ambition that has motivated Western culture to challenge every limitation on its creativity. In ancient philosophy, the infinite was that which lacked determinate form and was therefore beyond human understanding. In modern philosophy, infinity came to refer instead to the immeasurable expanse of the universe. Spengler's symbol combined both views into a powerful anthropology. Faustian man, Spengler boasted, discovers his own potentialities in confronting an unbounded universe of unlimited possibilities. He strives to see all things in relation to the highest or most distant horizons, which, in turn, he seeks to surpass and extend.

Spengler was not a fascist, but his anthropology pulsed with its tropes. The souls of Faustian men (and they were all men) make them visionaries, creators, and discoverers. They write treatises to explore their souls, build ships to explore the earth, and invent telescopes to explore the heavens.[21] Today, European men might be accountants, laborers, or service workers. But in their souls, Spengler told them, they are pioneers, builders, and conquerors of time, space, and human subjectivity. Faustian men are always preternaturally *more:* more creative, more daring, more individualistic, more heroic, more ambitious, more restless, more demanding, more lethal, more self-denying. Spengler's conceit was that Western culture is the product of this surpassing ambition to challenge human finitude. It is propelled by an ethic that encourages the loftiest human personalities. Like other cultures, the West has its own morality; but unlike others, Spengler wrote, this morality requires the most severe self-sacrifice in pursuit of the most distant goals. This ethic has no claim to universal validity – it is not written in the hearts or natures of all human beings – yet its requirements have inspired all the giants and geniuses of the West. "The entire Faustian ethic is an '*excelsior*'—the fulfillment of an 'I,'" Spengler argued. "Here Luther is completely at one with Nietzsche, Popes with Darwinians, Socialists with Jesuits."[22]

Where did this heroic culture begin? Not with the birth of ancient Greece, the founding of Rome, or the emergence of Christianity. Spengler credited no preceding culture or outside influence for its conception. The Faustian West was something absolutely original, a completely new and unprecedented orientation to the world. It began mysteriously a millennium ago, "on the northern plains between the Elbe and Tagus," and gradually came to include all of Western Europe and most of North America.[23] Its first stirrings occurred with the blossoming of Romanesque architecture and Scholastic thought. A new culture was born, its confidence in human powers breaking decisively with the submissive mentality of the Magian peoples (the early Middle Ages being a part of the long twilight of antiquity). Institutionally, its springtime saw the strengthening of imperial authority and the reform of the papacy and monastic life. Intellectually, it saw the emergence of Aristotelian science, systematic theology, and theoretical precision in sacramental doctrine and penitential practice. Artistically, it entered young adulthood in Gothic architecture and the development of orchestral music, the highest arts of the Faustian soul.

Here then was the advent of a new man, the like of which was found nowhere else.[24] Spengler chronicled the great moments of Faustian culture. It reached a new age in the Reformation and the Baroque, when Faustian men broke through in fresh directions. The Reformation pushed its vitality inward, toward the interrogation of conscience and the pitiless examination of faith. Luther "completely liberated the Faustian personality" by eliminating priestly authority and making Faustian man responsible for his own salvation.[25] The Baroque expanded its soul outward. Its arts attempted to bend matter and stretch stone into visible expressions of infinity itself. As the West's technological power increased exponentially in modernity, its aesthetic energies began to plateau. In the Enlightenment, Spengler saw Faustian ambitions becoming more abstract. This was the era of scientific inquiry and the string quartet. The Enlightenment intensified, to an unrivaled degree, Faustian man's assault on nature. In the twentieth century, Spengler observed, humans live in a cultural autumn, an era in which the arts are largely exhausted – "of great painting or great music there can no longer be" – but the attempt to dominate the natural world continues.[26]

Spengler's theory of Western development challenged that of Max Weber, one of the few scholars who agreed to discuss *The Decline of the West* in an academic forum (Weber was respectful but critical in their 1920 meeting). Weber's theory posited that the West had charted a path of development that could be followed by other modernizing cultures. At its root was a process he named "rationalization." Weber attributed the explosive growth of Western power and productivity to the culture's enhanced aptitude to reason instrumentally and to create bureaucratic institutions, such as the rule of law and capitalist economies, that reflected its rational procedures. Spengler turned Weber's thesis on its head. Where Weber saw objectivity, restraint, and cold logic as the motive force of Western culture, Spengler saw passion, energy, and even daring irrationality. And where Weber saw a universal culture of impersonal rationality, Spengler saw a particular culture of personal striving.[27]

Spengler did not document the philosophical sources of his anthropology, but Hegel was likely an inspiration.[28] Like Kant before him and Nietzsche after, Hegel was impressed by the antagonistic and irascible drives that often spur human advancement (Kant called it our "asocial sociability"). Hegel's parable of the master and slave famously described an early phase of human development, in which the master's desire to win a battle for prestige over a slave is resolved by their agreement to recognize each other as equals. Spengler did not take Hegel as his guide to the meaning of history, but his vision of the Faustian soul clearly admired the qualities of Hegel's master. The aristocratic desire to perform great deeds, to attain the highest excellences, and above all, the willingness to risk everything in pursuit of immaterial goods – for Spengler these were the unique traits of Faustian culture.[29] Unlike Hegel, however, Spengler did not see this drive as dependent on a slave's recognition. He saw culture as an attempt to transcend nature, not to dominate others. And this aspiration was religious in nature – a faith that once impelled Faustian men to their greatest heights, but now sapped their most vital instincts.

Faustian Christianity

With his understanding of human identity in place, Spengler made a radical interpretation of Western Christianity, whose details he hid in the largely unread second volume of *The Decline of the West*. Born into a Protestant family, Spengler reported no moment of adult Christian faith, and his mature theological views unambiguously owed more to secular philosophy than to the Bible. When he wrote about God, Spengler described him as the impersonal power of nature, a view expressing a form of pantheism that figured controversially in nineteenth-century Germany. Although not a Christian or a theist in any traditional sense, Spengler's understanding of human identity was nonetheless fundamentally religious. He regarded all creative activity as an expression of religious feeling. "Every soul has religion," he observed, "all arts, doctrines, customs, all metaphysical and mathematical form-worlds, all ornament, every column and verse and idea – are ultimately religious."[30]

No reader of *The Decline of the West* can avoid being struck by its overwhelming focus on Christian thought and culture, as well as its impressive command of Christian theology. The book was in many ways a record of its author's intellectual and aesthetic enthusiasms, virtually all of which came from the Christianity of the high Middle Ages, Renaissance, and Baroque.[31] Christianity was at the center of Western identity. Spengler could not have been clearer on this point, or on his rejection of Christian doctrine. He did not offer a Christian account of the rise of the West. Rather, he demolished any such argument. It was among the most revealing and significant aspects of the work. He did not argue that there is no Western civilization without Christianity. He argued that there is no Christianity without Western civilization. He arrived at this conclusion, as we began to see, by claiming the West began with the birth of Scholasticism, Gothic architecture, and polyphony. Here was the springtime not only of a new man, but of a new Faustian religion as well. Its theologians attempted to unlock the secrets of nature through dialectic, and its priests labored to wring the truth from God through prayer.[32] Its intellectual and artistic achievements were not testimonies to faith in God. They were the monuments of Faustian man's attempt – in speculation, marble, glass, and music – to propel himself into infinity. Spengler surveyed Western painting, sculpture, and architecture. The angelic hierarchies, the haloed saints and scholars, the heaven-thrusting spires, and the worship of a deified man – what are these, Spengler asked, if not the attempt of Faustian men to depict their heroic yearning for infinity?[33]

"It was not Christianity that transformed Faustian man," Spengler wrote in a critical passage, "but Faustian man who transformed Christianity."[34] Faustian man had the strength to make Christianity his own, turning a formerly world-rejecting faith into a world-transforming doctrine. In the minds and hands of Europeans, Christianity subdued the unearthly utopianism of its earliest believers, becoming a religion that affirmed the expansion of human freedom, power, and knowledge. Spengler implied that for Faustian men there is no biblical god, but there is high Christian culture, which is a tribute to *his* identity. Spengler thereby transformed Western Christianity from a universal creed into a tribal signifier. He was an atheist who regarded Christianity as a religion indigenous to Europe. His death in 1936 meant he would not live to see Christianity's waning in Europe or its expansion into the "colored" world of the global South. But it permitted him to argue, in a strange anticipation of postcolonial theory, that Western Christianity was the communal self-worship of people of European descent.

But Spengler also charged modern Christianity with playing an important role in Western decline. No longer able to summon Europeans to transformative goals, it now weakens its host culture through its moral teachings. Spengler portrayed early Christianity as a primitive socialism inspired by a Semitic longing for a better world. His view of Christianity was not Nietzschean – Spengler had a vastly more positive a view of its earthly achievements – but his view of its influence on modern politics was.[35] He regarded liberal political ideals as the secular offspring of a purer and more ancient form of Christian faith that had partly reemerged in modernity. They were what remained of Christian piety after it had lost faith in its doctrinal claims, and instead offered moral support to the cause of human equality. Liberalism "detests every kind of greatness, everything that towers, rules, is superior," Spengler complained.[36] *The Decline of the West* included an anguished commentary on the life of Jesus. Its purpose, it seems, was to exonerate Jesus of the leveling moralism that inspired modern social reformers. Spengler praised his "pure religiousness" that was indifferent to world-improvement. Spengler's Jesus was concerned only with a supersensible world, and showed no interest in bringing justice or peace to this one – "to ascribe social purposes to Jesus is a blasphemy."[37] Yet Spengler did not hide his distaste of modern Christians who believed otherwise, and he castigated missionaries for spreading its teachings to the encroaching "colored" world. For Spengler, Christianity was simultaneously the West's greatest achievement – and its deepest ailment.[38]

Winter Is Coming

For all its vitality, Faustian culture is still mortal. As Spengler envisioned its final season, he predicted the rise of democratic "Caesars," growing racial animosity, and even environmental crises, due to rampant technological exploitation of nature. Who will give birth to the next great culture? Perhaps Russia, he hinted, which had yet to birth an authentic culture, but might do so after it renounced Bolshevism and renewed its own Christian traditions (Lenin despised Spengler's book, and for good reason).[39] As for Americans and Europeans, Spengler urged them to meet their fate like an unrelieved Roman soldier at Pompeii – defiant, unbending, and undeceived about their inevitable doom.

Winter is therefore coming, but it will not arrive for a few centuries. Where are Europe and America headed in the last season of life? Spengler offered clues in his speculative chronologies, which in some editions were illustrated with elaborate timelines comparing the rise and fall of cultures. *The Decline of the West* put forward an implicit comparison of the Faustian West and ancient Rome. It suggested that the liberal West had reached a life-age that corresponded to the fall of the Republic, rather than the fall of the Empire. Spengler described the last days of liberalism as a time of "civilization" that would see, as did the aging Roman state, the mixing of peoples and the moving of borders. His short 1931 book *Man and Technics* voiced the fear that the tools of Western science and technology, shared with the developing world in a moment of myopia, would be used against the West in a coming iron age.[40] The imperium is slowly petrifying, yet it can survive for a time if it secures its technological supremacy and prevents the flow of global immigration. In his last published piece, a short column sent to an American newspaper, Spengler warned against political idealism and counseled that the future would belong to the race that remained "strong" in the face of competitors.[41]

It was a final return to a theme he failed to resolve. Spengler never got clear on the relationship between race and culture, and he left in place a dangerous ambiguity. On the one hand, Spengler's decision, in his own moment of trial, was to reject Nazi doctrines and racial anti-Semitism. Across his work he took a strong stand against the fiction of racial purism and the folly of racial preservationism. In *The Hour of Decision* he wrote:

> Race purity is a grotesque word in view of the fact that for centuries all stocks and species have been mixed, and that warlike—that is, healthy—generations with a future before them have from time immemorial always welcomed a stranger into the family if he had "race," to whatever race it was he belonged. Those who talk too much about race no longer have it in them.[42]

To the disappointment of the racist right, Spengler was therefore not a "race realist." He did not think racial groups were natural kinds, nor did he believe that they formed distinct sub-species. Although profound differences separated peoples and cultures forever, "a strict classification of races is impossible."[43]

On the other hand, Spengler was a source of regret to Nazi propagandists and even to Hitler himself, and not entirely without reason.[44] In the early years of Weimar, Spengler was aligned with the Conservative Revolution. His contributions to this movement, chiefly his 1919 manifesto *Prussianism and Socialism*, imagined a special path for Germany that avoided the errors of liberalism and communism. To the Nazis, his views were promising. Spengler was for hierarchy against equality, for order against anarchy, for war against peace, and for passion against reason. Most important, his argument that language, history, and geography are so deeply impressed on human identities that they create fundamentally divergent ways of life seemed an obvious precursor to the young Nazi movement. Spengler came to disagree with it, yet he struggled to explain that if culture was rooted in a certain soil and landscape, it nonetheless transcended race. In the end, he found himself in an intellectual no man's land, arguing that peoples have their own collective consciousness, as it were, but not an identity rooted in a shared heredity.[45]

Spengler believed the crisis of the West consisted in confusion about its identity and uncertainty about its civilizational purpose. He wrote to restore both: to find an identity that could not be lost and a purpose in which all could be united. Although a radical conservative, he glimpsed the shape of one possible world after liberalism. He foresaw an age where people compete for the recognition of their group differences, rather than demand the recognition of their individual similarities; where they seek to know not only what binds them to certain groups, but what distinguishes them from others. To a generation tired of multicultural pieties, but knowing no others, his message is seductive. It says, "This heroic culture is your inheritance, and yours alone. You stand in a line of men who have attained the highest excellences and freely endured the hardest challenges. Albert the Great, Cortés, Shakespeare, Bacon, the Wright Brothers all carry this daring spirit, and so do you."

Spengler's understanding of human identity was profoundly illiberal, but it remains tempting for that very reason. He alleviates the burden of giving form to one's soul through reflection, discipline, and choice, telling us that identity must be accepted as part of an unchosen destiny. In this respect, Spengler refuted himself, arguing for what he otherwise claimed was impossible. He applied his learning to proposing a cultural identity that others could freely choose for themselves, a vision of human life that individuals could share in only through individual acts of thought and choice. But his inconsistencies are essential to his lasting allure, and we are obtuse if we cannot imagine both its appeal and its danger. To learn that one is the inheritor of a great patrimony is ennobling. To learn that it is received through birth is consoling. But to be told that it destines one to permanent alienation from others – that is to tempt catastrophe. Spengler did not regard his work as a success, and in the final years of his life, after being intimidated by the tyranny he bravely betrayed, he retreated into the study of archaic civilizations, sketching drafts of speculative histories that would not be published until after his death at age fifty-seven. To understand the future seemingly required going back before the birth of the West, back even before the dawn of recorded time. It was a path followed by Spengler's most influential translator, Julius Evola.

Chapter 2

THE FANTASIST

In early October 1951, Julius Evola was carried on a stretcher into Rome's Palace of Justice, where he would stand trial for promoting the restoration of the dissolved Fascist Party. He had been held in the Regina Coeli prison since April, and the trial, which would end with his exoneration, helped to secure his reputation as an intellectual pariah in postwar Italy. The courtroom was filled with young men, many of them war veterans, who looked to the paraplegic defendant as the leader of an intransigent Italian right. Although he had denied the legitimacy of the Italian state in writing, Evola was respectful of the court, whom he addressed while wearing his trademark monocle.

In his statement of self-defense, Evola acknowledged his sympathies for Italian fascism, but reminded the court that he had never joined the Fascist Party and had written critically of its policies, at some danger to himself. Admitting he had been an "ideological accessory" to anti-liberal movements, he testified that his involvement took place on a "purely intellectual and doctrinal level." Evola struck a pose of philosophical detachment, explaining that he defended timeless principles that transcended any political regime. "I have defended, and I still defend, fascist ideas, not inasmuch as they are 'fascist,'" he stated, "but in the measure that they revive ideas superior and anterior to fascism." Evola protested that his principles were those shared universally before the French Revolution, and that if his opinions were criminal, then Plato, Aristotle, and Dante should be seated next to him.[1]

Evola had been arrested along with thirty other conspirators, variously charged with promoting political sedition and terrorism. Among the evidence presented against him was a magazine essay published in 1950 entitled "Guidelines." One of his first responses to the changed political realities in Europe, the manifesto argued for the founding of a radical right that could stand apart from the emerging liberal order. It called for a group animated by a "Legionary spirit" that exemplified hierarchical and aristocratic values during a time of bourgeois decadence. Evola noted that the essay never endorsed violence or proposed the formation of a political party. It called instead for a "spiritual revolution" of a new elite that could prepare the ground for postliberal regimes on the European continent. After a two-month trial, the court declared Evola innocent. In a letter to Carl Schmitt shortly after the verdict, Evola seemed confident of his future in public life and boasted that the trial had provided "free publicity in my favor."[2]

In fact, the trial was one of the last times Evola would leave his nearby apartment until his death in 1974, and he later lamented that it had permanently blackened his reputation. He had been paralyzed in March 1945 while going for a walk during an Allied bombing run in Vienna, where he was living under a false name after escaping police detention in Rome (Evola said he was following his rule "to seek dangers as a tacit way of putting fate to the test").[3] But even as an invalid he could not avoid being linked to violent extremism. He continued to be regarded as the leading theorist of Italian neo-fascism, and his work would be associated with (and sometimes cited by) terrorist groups throughout Italy's "Years of Lead," a period of three decades, ending only in the early 1980s, that saw a string of bombings by right-wing activists pursuing a "strategy of tension" in face of a perceived Communist threat. A 1985 government report after a bombing in Bologna identified Evola as an "inspiration" and "one of the gurus of the Italian extreme right."[4]

Painter, occultist, mountaineer, sexologist, and unreliable scholar of Eastern religions, Evola was one of the strangest intellectual figures of his century. He impressed Benito Mussolini, worried Heinrich Himmler, and fascinated Corneliu Codreanu. Umberto Eco mocked him, the future Pope Paul VI condemned him, and Steve Bannon named him as an influence. Over a publishing career of more than fifty years, Evola produced an astonishing stream of books and articles that never deviated from what he called "the great political tradition of the European Right." His vision was uniquely utopian. It was a utopianism of the extreme right, and one that pitilessly inverted the ideals of liberal modernity. Against a secular world of growing freedom and equality, he conjured a fantastic world of his own imagination – a sacred world of unchanging order and inequality, in which all authority was absolute and every activity was holy. Evola aspired to be the most right-wing thinker possible in the modern world. There was nobody to his right, he believed, nor could there be.[5]

Idealism and the Absolute Individual

Giulio Cesare Andrea Evola was born in Rome on May 19, 1898, to a Sicilian family with distant ties to nobility. He responded to the title "baron" and adopted the name Julius to emphasize his spiritual connection to Roman antiquity. About his background little is known. No biographer has undertaken the project, and Evola carefully hid the details of his personal life, which he regarded as irrelevant to his work. From his autobiography, we learn only what he had already revealed in previous writings, where he placed his early life in the context of a personal crisis following the First World War.

Evola served in an artillery unit during the conflict, and the experience left him, like many of his generation, disoriented and open to new modes of thinking. When he first achieved public notice in his early twenties, it was for his artistic talents. As a painter, Evola was a leading figure of the Dadaist movement in Italy, his work enjoying exhibitions in Milan and Berlin. Some of his paintings, which he described as "inner landscapes," can be viewed at major European museums even today. As a poet, Evola wrote in French, occasionally reading his poems in cabarets while accompanied by the music of Schoenberg, Bartók, and Satie. Evola never repented of his avant-garde phase and its attack on middle-class manners and culture. Yet it ended abruptly, he claimed, when the spiritual emptiness of modern life brought him to contemplate suicide.[6]

Evola's crisis was the most personally revealing moment in his life, and it inspired him to seek ideas that remained fundamental for his mature political work. In 1922, he underwent what he called a "conversion," in which his desire to end his life was overcome by studying an early Buddhist text. Evola did not become a Buddhist, but he credited Theravada teachings with providing an "illumination" as to how he could remain in the world while not being compromised by it. He claimed that Buddhism, in its true form, is not a religion, and has nothing to do with an ethics of compassion and human equality. Buddhism is "Roman" and "aristocratic" because it enables one to transcend the needs and concerns of normal human beings. Those with the strength to develop self-mastery attain what he called the "Unconditioned," which is not an escape from this world, but a state of superiority over it. In a book he wrote to pay his "debt" to the Buddha, Evola explained that Buddhism taught him "each individual must rely on himself, and on his own exertions, just as a soldier who is lost must rely on himself alone to rejoin the marching army."[7]

For much of the next decade, Evola sought to make philosophical sense of his experience through a study of German Idealism. He labored to explain himself in *Theory of the Absolute Individual* (1927) and *Phenomenology of the Absolute Individual* (1930), books that were his first and only attempts to win a mainstream scholarly audience.[8] They targeted Giovanni Gentile, who was arguably the most influential Idealist philosopher of the time, as well as the principal theorist of the young fascist movement in Italy. The books represented an unsuccessful bid for attention from both the university and the regime of Mussolini, whose March on Rome in 1922 had inaugurated its twenty years in power. Evola believed that Idealism was the greatest of the Western philosophical systems, but that its failure, and hence the failure of all philosophy, revealed the need for radically different accounts of knowledge and political life.

Idealism explained the human mind's relationship with reality by arguing that being is the product of thought—that what the intellect knows is, strictly speaking, its own cognitive activity. Evola was impressed by Idealism's striving for intellectual self-sufficiency ("the world can only be *my* world," he affirmed), but he argued that it left the deepest human problems unsolved. Its mistake was to leave the human mind passively withdrawn into itself, alienated from real life and concrete experience. It was not enough to make the "Absolute Ego" the ground of all experience, Evola wrote. The "Absolute Individual" must affirm himself as the ground of all meaning. Evola called his position "Magical Idealism." What he meant was made clear in a 1927 essay, which announced that the purpose of philosophy is not to acquire theoretical knowledge at all. Its purpose is radical self-transformation – it is to transform a student into a self-directed rather than an other-directed person, into a being who can create and control their own reality, rather than being conditioned by it.[9]

Evola's brand of Idealism found few readers and fewer converts, and he soon realized he had failed in reconciling individual liberation with true freedom in the world. He believed that he found a more promising path, however, with the help of a friend, Arturo Reghini, who recommended the writings of a French scholar named René Guénon. Guénon had experienced a personal crisis much like Evola's, and he shared Evola's growing interest in spiritualism and the occult. His work purported to explain, as Idealism could not, what kind of society exemplified the inegalitarian values that Evola glimpsed in his conversion. It was a community in which human beings continued to live in the uninterrupted tranquility of sacred order, and in which uncertainty and disagreement find no place. Evola had located his lost army. Guénon called it the world of "Tradition," and its discovery was the most important intellectual event in Evola's life, leading him away from academic philosophy and into the politics of fascist Europe.

The World of Tradition

Evola remarked that encountering Guénon was like acquiring eyes and ears, enabling him to perceive what had previously been invisible and mute. He called Guénon his "master," a title that obscured the intellectual distance between them, as well as Evola's greater originality as a thinker. Guénon was a convert to Islam who had moved from Paris to Cairo in 1930, in search of a more traditional society. Sometimes called the "Descartes of esotericism," he was an influential exponent of "traditionalism," a school of thought that sought to identify the higher principles shared by the world's great spiritual teachers. Guénon's books claimed to reveal the "Primal Tradition" behind these traditions, whose single inner core he distinguished from its various outer expressions. Evola was less interested in Guénon's work in comparative religion than his understanding of modernity, which offered Evola a powerful explanation for his own spiritual anomie. In his 1927 book *The Crisis of the Modern World* Guénon argued that modernity marked the final stage of a millennia-long cycle of historical decline. Those in the West live in what Hinduism calls the Kali Yuga, a spiritual dark age in which knowledge of "transcendence" has been almost entirely lost.[10]

Evola now saw the modern world in a striking new way: it was the result of a fractured relationship with a transcendent realm of order, which had unleashed social chaos and uncertainty. He organized his thoughts in his most famous work, *Revolt Against the Modern World,* a book that has enjoyed a cult-like status for the radical right since its publication in 1934. Evola was raised in a Catholic family, and his diagnosis of contemporary life often sounded Christian, which it emphatically was not. The basic problem with modernity is "desacralization," the collapse of spiritual meaning in daily life. Work, family, leisure, and citizenship are no longer saturated with spiritual importance, but are understood in functionally secular terms. "Man, like never before, has lost every possibility of contact with metaphysical reality," Evola wrote, because materialism "kills every possibility, deflects every intent, and paralyzes every attempt" at aspiring to a higher form of life.[11]

Following Guénon, Evola traced the disorders of modernity to its loss of contact with Tradition, which he interpreted in political terms. Astonishingly, he did not date the break to the Enlightenment, the Reformation, or the end of antiquity. No, the world has been slouching into spiritual poverty since the eighth century BC, when the world of Tradition began to disappear, just as historical consciousness began to dawn. *Revolt* was an epic, deadly serious, and occasionally surreal attempt to summon this vanished world and unearth its hidden clues in later history. It spurned the conventions of historical scholarship entirely, claiming that Tradition could be accessed only by way of myth, legend, and esoteric readings of premodern texts. It contained, for example, an appendix on Arthurian legends and the Holy Grail, to which Evola added reflections on alchemy, all of which he identified as sources of hermetic knowledge. Evola's sources, however fantastic, were secondary to his primary purpose, which was to enchant readers with the magical world of human prehistory.[12]

Revolt contended that primordial societies all operated on the same principles. The truths of Tradition are simple and few, varying only in expression. In a traditional culture, every aspect of human life, every social activity, role, and caste, is dedicated to the service of a higher order; indeed, they are ritual pathways into what Evola deceptively called "transcendence." There is no person or office whose duties are not prescribed, and thus consecrated, by its place in a hierarchy believed to be an earthly reflection of a celestial order. Evola claimed that this idea informed Norse poetry, Hindu scripture, Roman religion, Celtic legend, and Mesoamerican myth – all attest to a social order where human beings find their place and purpose living under sacred hierarchy. Evola contrasted his view with that of Spengler, whose work he translated into Italian. Spengler's flaw was that he "lacked any understanding of metaphysics and transcendence," which led him to conclude that cultures were irreducibly different. Evola studied Spengler closely and agreed with the German's aristocratic sensibilities, but arrived at a different conclusion, arguing that there are timeless and universal principles that have provided the foundation for every traditional culture.[13]

The world of Tradition differs from the world of modernity in fundamental respects. Because the "man of tradition" is preternaturally aware of a superior dimension of existence, he experiences nature, history, and society in altogether different ways. He follows what Evola called the "doctrine of two natures." He values the absolute over the contingent, the invisible over the visible, the sacred over the profane, and being over becoming. Evola's doctrine was metaphysically simple. For the follower of Tradition, the phenomenal realm of daily experience is supported, sustained, and animated by a higher spiritual realm. "In the traditional world," Evola explained, "nature was not thought about but lived as though it were a great, sacred, animated body, the visible expression of the invisible."[14] Evola possessed a command of ancient and modern philosophy, but he declined, at every opportunity, to offer a philosophical defense of his doctrine. The "demon of dialectics" cannot demonstrate truths that can be perceived only by an elect few who are disposed by nature to see them. But the doctrine, treated as incontestably true, allowed Evola to make a fascinating interpretation of traditional life and its deepest purposes.

Tradition endowed human pursuits with absolute meaning. It did so by transforming them into rites. Evola claimed to show how basic human activities – from eating and sex, commerce and games, to war and social intercourse – were elevated by Tradition into something ritualistic, becoming activities whose very repetitiveness offered a glimpse of an unchanging eternal realm. He did not argue that Tradition is "religious," and he strongly denied, for reasons that will be made clear, that it corresponds to our notions of religious belief. Human beings must eat, mate, fight, die, play, and obey – and it was the purpose of Tradition to turn these mortal necessities into holy occasions. Tradition thereby protected human beings, healing the gap between their understanding of the social world and its fearful complexity. Evola's profound suggestion was that Tradition shelters human beings from the ravages of mortality, change, and contingency. It was his most humane insight and his most deeply felt problem. Human life is threatened by direct exposure to its own impermanence, and all societies are horrified by their own extinction. Tradition offers protection from the terror of time, creating islands of unchanging order in a sea of flux and decay. In a revealing phrase, Evola spoke of Tradition as a "force that consumes time and history."[15]

Tradition is therefore the triumph of order over chaos. Yet the triumph requires human effort, and without the active imposition of "form," the "matter" of human life inevitably degenerates. At the heart of Evola's work was a defense of the sacrality of political authority. The hierarchy of nature will collapse and the healing of time will fail, he maintained, if not guarded by transcendent authority. Evola looked into the past and saw what modernity, in its blindness and hubris, could no longer perceive: true power and authority always come from above, never from below. "According to Tradition," he imagined, "every authority is fraudulent, every law unjust, every institution is vain and ephemeral unless they are derived from above and oriented upward."[16] True authority is therefore always absolute and beyond challenge. It does not rely on brute coercion or violence, however, nor does its legitimacy rest on popular consent. As an "incursion" from a realm beyond mere life, the traditional state possessed what Evola called "anagogic" power. It inspired obedience, rooted in a kind of awe, due to its ability "to lead man from the lower order of reality to the higher."[17]

Revolt Against the Modern World invoked nearly every antimodern trope. There was once harmony, but now there is disorder. There was once community, but now there is loneliness. There was once happiness, but now there is misery. Yet Evola warned against the fantasy of escaping modernity for an imagined golden age. His books were written not to comfort the lost soldiers of Tradition, but to provide "ideological guidance" for those with a realistic view of future possibilities.[18] His battle myth, which he refined over decades, was that the decadent conditions of modernity imposed new obligations on the invisible army of Tradition. Guénon had instructed his disciples to retreat into spiritual inwardness, in order to protect the superiority of the contemplative life over the active life. Evola broke with his master. "The spiritual and social conditions that characterize the Kali Yuga decrease the effectiveness of purely intellectual, contemplative, and ritual paths," he contended. "In this age of decadence, the only way open to those seeking the great liberation is one of action."[19]

Fascism, Racism, and the Crisis of Democratic Authority

In Tradition, Evola discovered the vantage point from which the deceptive "circle" of modernity could be transcended and seen for what it truly is. He saw it as the antithesis of everything that gave human life meaning. Drawing from Nietzsche's parable about the death of God, he described it as a historical process, developing over centuries, by which life had been slowly drained of transcendent significance. That "God is dead" did not mean that human beings had ceased calling themselves believers or worshipping. It meant that the spiritual values which once sustained the entire social order had collapsed, leaving behind structures that are "residues, empty shells, incapable of offering real support."[20]

For Evola, this crisis was not religious, and he did not mourn the death of a God he never believed in. The crisis of modernity was one of political authority. He identified its origin with liberalism, from which the evils of individualism, materialism, and egalitarianism inevitably followed. History is the battleground between Form and Matter, and its present belligerents are the defenders of Tradition and the tribunes of liberalism. Evola set them in absolute opposition. If Tradition defended the sacred, immaterial, and eternal, liberalism exalted the human, earthly, and mutable. If Tradition ordered life from above, liberalism emancipated it from below. Evola rarely cited intellectual authorities, and he never named, let alone examined, major philosophers in the liberal tradition. But Evola understood something important about liberalism, arguing that it transformed human life through a radical moral appeal.

Liberalism demanded that political authority and social inequalities require special justification. The philosophical differences between Locke, Rousseau, and Mazzini are unimportant, Evola implied, when compared to their shared suspicion of traditional authority. Liberalism submits social hierarchies to popular scrutiny, rather than shielding them from it. Its deepest principle is that authority flows from below to above, and that a ruler is legitimate only when ratified by the consent of the ruled. Evola was horrified by the "anti-traditional" character of liberalism, especially its desire to free individuals from relationships of command and obedience. Everything he revered – social castes, natural inequalities, and sacred privileges – was targeted by liberalism for reform or abolition. He regarded the founding of the Italian Republic in 1871 as a calamity, but saved his harshest criticisms for the United States. It was a place where "anyone can be anyone he wants to be" and "each person can presume to possess the potential of everyone else," he complained. Worst of all, "the terms 'superior' and 'inferior' lose their meaning."[21]

Evola sharpened his critique of liberalism in the years leading up to the Second World War, during which he edited a series of right-wing magazines and newspapers, including the influential *Il regime fascista*. He argued that liberalism is false to human nature and blind to human experience. It conceives of human beings as individual bearers of rights, who can define and pursue for themselves an understanding of the good life. But the law of life is inequality, Evola argued, and most human beings are born to obey, not to rule. They find happiness and dignity in the comforting continuities of Tradition, not in the unending debates of parliamentary democracy. Liberalism is perniciously disorienting. By encouraging people to think and act apart from the guidance of authority, it renders them unable to see the naturalness, goodness, and even beauty in long-standing customs and inequalities. "Freedom can only exist when there are masters opposed to slaves," Evola protested, "when there are proud leaders and followers that boldly and generously put their lives and destinies in their hands."[22]

Evola's writings showed the influence of Joseph de Maistre and Juan Donoso Cortés, reactionaries who also mourned the disruption of European social patterns by revolutionary ideals. But unlike them Evola was not a Christian, and his criticisms owed more to Roman antiquity than to Roman Catholicism. He argued that a liberal political order is not only inhumane – it is an impossibility. It is impossible, that is, for liberal rulers to act consistently with their stated principles. All political authority rests on judgments and exercises of power that cannot be justified by liberal norms. Liberalism fantastically overestimates the human capacity to justify *any* authority, entertaining the delusion that people can follow laws they author, venerate customs they can change, and obey sovereigns they can depose. Evola concluded that liberalism is not even a degenerate form of politics. It is an anti-politics, an anarchic form of life marked by the absence of true power in public life. And as there was no intellectual solution to its crisis of authority, Evola looked about for a "revolution from above."[23]

Evola was never a committed fascist. "Fascism is not enough," he wrote, adding that he hoped for a movement "more radical, more intrepid, a fascism that is truly absolute."[24] His courtroom claim that he had been targeted by supporters of Mussolini's regime was truthful; his criticisms of its tactics and style even made it necessary to retain bodyguards. But in fascism, Evola also sensed a rare opening to the world of Tradition. He was impressed by Mussolini's argument that the state created the nation (rather than the other way around) and his invocation of the symbol of imperial Rome. Mussolini had taken notice of Evola by the late 1920s, and it was to guide the regime that Evola authored his only major wartime book, *Synthesis of the Doctrine of Race* (1941), which proposed the "rectification" of Fascist policy by the higher perspective of Tradition.[25]

Racism expressed a healthy revulsion to the "regression of castes," Evola's term for the subversion of hierarchy and rank in modern societies. But its biological "fetishism" reflected a reductive view of human beings. Evola distinguished between three different kinds of race – body, spirit, and soul – and argued for the absolute priority of the spiritual over the biological. One's "spiritual race," as he termed it, is revealed in one's intellectual attitude and outlook, with those of a "higher" race being innately oriented to properly spiritual concerns, making them naturally fit to command. His views built on an earlier historical work, *The Myth of the Blood* (1937), and mixed ideas from Plato and Eastern religions in suggesting that individual identities are inborn, fixed, and possibly reflect a pre-mortal existence. To be born into a certain condition, as a man or a woman, in one social class and family rather than another, and with certain talents and dispositions, he argued, reflected one's destiny.[26] Evola did not have enlightened views on race – his opinions of African Americans and Jews were reprehensible – but he did not embrace scientific racism and wrote critically of its proponents, at some cost to his public reputation. In the event, his writings exercised little influence on state policy, and he eventually concluded that Italian fascism had been a "joke." In a 1964 review of the regime, he argued that its legitimate aspirations were compromised by the character of the Italian people.[27]

Evola alleged the opposite occurred in Germany, where a healthy culture, founded on duty and obedience to authority, was corrupted by a perverse ideology and a demagogic leader.[28] *Revolt* had been quickly translated into German and was favorably received by groups affiliated with the Conservative Revolution. Evola visited Germany throughout the 1930s, giving lectures to conservative social clubs.[29] He formed an ambivalent view of the new regime. Like Spengler, he criticized Nazi ideology from the right, lamenting its "proletarian aspect" and the absence of aristocratic traits in Hitler. He also questioned its views on race, writing in 1931 that a nation could not be properly founded on an ideal of ethnic purity.[30] But in the Third Reich Evola saw positive developments as well. He was captivated by the SS and imagined in Himmler's organization the seeds of a true ruling class – an elite "Order," as he named it, based on an austere code and animated by a spirituality connecting it to ancient Rome. Little is known for certain about Evola's involvement with the regime or about his visits to eastern Europe, where he met with leaders of the Romanian Iron Guard. He published little, but his elitism seems to have raised concerns. An SS report warned that Evola was a "reactionary Roman" whose "ultimate and secret motivation . . . must be sought in a revolt of the old aristocracy."[31]

A Real Right for Real Men

After the war, Evola withdrew to his Rome apartment, where, supported by a military pension and a wealthy benefactor, he committed himself to preserving the principles of what he called the "real right." He mourned the destructiveness of the conflict but declared himself innocent of complicity with its atrocities, claiming he had never known of them. The tragedy of European fascism, he maintained, was that it imitated the ideologies to which it was allegedly opposed. It claimed legitimacy through popular support and sought unity through common identity. He drew the striking conclusion, fatal to any remaining public respectability, that fascism was not a moral catastrophe for the illiberal right. The "real right" had not failed – it had never been tried.

In his 1953 book *Man Among the Ruins,* Evola outlined a political program for creating a postliberal right. Its strategy guided his postwar writing and exercised an extensive influence on the European radical right. Evola's stature began to rise again and he attracted younger readers. He set to attacking mainstream conservative parties, charging that Western nations lacked genuine right-wing movements and featured parties of the left exclusively. "Today there is very little that deserves to be preserved," he argued, and parties of the so-called right are largely to blame.[32] They offer no resistance to liberal ideals, supporting capitalism and bourgeois morality as bulwarks of individual liberty. For Evola, everything depended on recognizing the fundamental agreement between liberalism, socialism, and communism: each celebrated human liberation from traditional constraints, disagreeing only about the best means of achieving it. His views became darker as he argued that Americanism and communism were "two tongs of the same pincers," since they pointed to the same standardizing and leveling outcomes.[33]

Evola's hope lay in the restoration of a "real right." A "real right" is not an ideological movement, he explained, and it advances no partisan agenda. It defends a view of life based on higher principles that transcend the economic plane entirely. Evola drew revealing comparisons with the French and Communist revolutions, which were also inspired by precise doctrinal formulations. But unlike modern ideologies, Evola held, a "real right" defends spiritual principles that are timeless, unchanging, absolute, and metahistorical. At the center of its "majestic affirmations" is a defense of the sacrality of temporal authority. All ordered societies require institutions that provide absolute "form" amid their changing material features, and it is the purpose of a real right to defend the authorities, classes, and customs by which human life is "drawn upward." Evola did not provide a detailed picture of this postliberal order, which seemed to combine elements of sacred kingship and imperial Rome (but rejected, he insisted, both totalitarianism and populist dictatorship). What was paramount was the principle that only a transformative leader could elevate humanity out of its degraded state. Such a leader could not appeal directly to the masses – that was the vulgar mistake of fascism – but must inspire submission through a lofty contempt for democratic norms and popular tastes. "The presence of superior individuals bestows on a multitude a meaning and a justification they previously lacked."[34]

But Evola's movement had practical aims as well, and here his strategy became worrisome to authorities and appealing to extremists. A "real right" cannot be restored by democratic means – no authority can be conferred from below to above – but a small vanguard can be initiated into its intransigent truths and prepared to follow a leader who embodies them. Evola's postwar writings addressed what he called "differentiated men," who felt they did not inwardly belong in liberal societies.[35] He appealed to them as men of superior integrity, honor, courage, and virility – men who were "ready for action" and capable of resisting every compromise and collaboration with liberalism. Evola did not envision a political party, but something more like a fraternal order that functioned as network for meta-political organization. Publishing houses, social clubs, and cultural foundations, he speculated, could somehow connect Europe's remaining aristocratic families with dispossessed members of the working class. Such a group would not make a long march through Western institutions. Evola dreamed that it might seize power during a democratic crisis, instituting a "New Order" from above.[36]

Evola's fantasies revealed something fundamental to his thought that he worked to keep obscure. From Plato to the Scholastics, philosophers in the West agreed that social hierarchies ought to reflect natural inequalities between human beings. While Evola aligned himself with this tradition, his views departed from it significantly.

His appeal to the "doctrine of two natures" did not reflect a belief in a higher metaphysical order of reality. Despite his criticisms of modern science, he accepted a cosmology that left no place for the supernatural. Evola's doctrine instead reflected a belief in two kinds of human beings, whose natures embodied fundamentally different modes of reality. Masters are those who grasp the fact that human beings must give shape and structure to life through the imposition of form. Those Aristotle called slaves do not grasp the nature of these higher principles, depending on the benevolent coercion of their superiors to give form to the chaos around and within them. Evola flattered himself that he and his students were distinguished by their knowledge of human differences, and hence by their exceptional capacities. They were those meant to rule, not meant to obey.

In 1961 Evola published his last major work, *Ride the Tiger,* a book that addressed the emerging counterculture of the decade. He admitted the failure of his earlier political strategies, acknowledging the seemingly insuperable obstacles to mobilizing a traditional right in Europe or North America. He counseled the practice of "apoliteia," a path of disengagement by which one could survive the dangers of liberalism without actively fleeing from them. For the first time, Evola engaged respectfully with intellectuals on the left, including Sartre, Camus, and writers of the Beat movement. He warned his army of "differentiated men" not to confuse their own radicalism with growing protests against bourgeois decadence. But the alienated students of the 1960s, he also wrote, were open to revolutionary perspectives, and Tradition might offer answers to the questions posed by existentialism, Freudianism, and even Marxism.[37]

Evola's thoughts grew apocalyptic, and he began to wonder if the decline of liberal society should be actively accelerated, rather than simply withstood. Since modern political institutions lack any higher legitimacy, he hinted, it might be "better to contribute to the fall of that which is already wavering."[38] Evola never explicitly called for violence in writing, but he signaled that the constraints of conventional morality were artificial and did not apply to the followers of Tradition. He contemplated the possibility of taking the "Left-Hand Path," an idea that he discovered in his early studies of Tantrism, but now put to ideological uses. Its original meaning referred to the careful use of normally forbidden things with a view to achieving a mystical experience (e.g., drugs and sex). Evola proposed that the "Left-Hand Path" might now include destructive and even criminal activity, when undertaken by those with a mature spiritual orientation. If the modern world represents the negation of Tradition, the "negation of the negation" could prove to be the "formative action" that opens space for the return of Tradition. Evola left it to his readers, and the small groups of students he hosted in his home, to draw the explosive conclusions.[39]

The Christian Schism

Evola anticipated the question whether a revived Christianity might foster a more traditional society and greater reverence for authority. He consistently denied that it could, offering arguments that shaped his intellectual legacy. Although avowedly spiritual, Evola was both a nonbeliever and openly hostile to Christianity, claiming to have rejected it in early youth after reading Russian literature. His first political book, *Pagan Imperialism* (1928), identified Christianity as an alien element in European culture, earning the censure of a future pope, Giovanni Battista Montini, in a Vatican newspaper. Evola later expressed embarrassment over its inflammatory style, but never retracted the substance of its criticisms, which recur throughout his work. "The greatest miracle of Christianity," he stated in a 1967 interview, "was succeeding in asserting itself among European peoples."[40]

Against pressure from religious traditionalists, Evola maintained that Christianity and Tradition are fundamentally irreconcilable. Christianity endangers the highest form of human wisdom, which depends on exceptional efforts at self-transformation. The Christian claim that wisdom is a gift from God, not the attainment of a superhuman elite, undercuts spiritual striving. It encourages dependency rather than ambition, gratitude rather than assurance, and passivity rather than daring. Christianity slanders as "Luciferian" all the "Faustian" virtues required to achieve true self-mastery.[41] Evola's spiritual interests varied widely over his career, but his lifelong interest in Christianity seemed to reflect a genuine quest for enlightenment. His 1963 autobiography included the fascinating report that during the 1930s he visited Catholic religious orders, spending time living with Benedictines, Carthusians, Cistercians, and Carmelites in search of an underground esoteric tradition in Christian monasticism. He was disappointed to find no "secret" teaching, he writes, only "moralistic" Catholic doctrine.[42]

Evola's deeper criticism was that Christianity is a solvent to political authority. Society needs to be governed by a spiritual authority, just as a human being must be governed by its soul (it is the error of liberalism to organize society around the needs of the body instead). But Evola denied that Christianity could provide this. Its cardinal heresy was that it divided spiritual and temporal power, clearly separating priestly and civil offices. For Evola, there was no more insidious idea in human history, and he traced virtually all the secularizing tendencies in liberal culture to Christianity's fateful separation of spiritual and temporal authority.[43] In dividing what belongs in perfect unity, it induces social schizophrenia, where no one authority possesses power over all human life. Evola insisted on the anomalous character of the Christian "schism" from Tradition, alleging that ancient Egyptian, Roman, Assyrian, Persian, and Hindu societies (indeed, seemingly every traditional society) united kingship and priesthood into a single office. He acknowledged that Christian history featured eras of close cooperation between church and state, and he wrote wistfully of failed medieval attempts to absorb the church into imperial authority. The war between "Ghibellines" and "Guelphs," as he called it, was the most momentous intellectual battle in Western history, pitting defenders of imperial supremacy against defenders of ecclesial liberty. Evola understood that as a "Ghibelline" he had lost, and the church had retained its institutional autonomy.[44]

Christianity is therefore the unhealed wound at the heart of Western culture. As a religion open to all people, regardless of status or background, it eroded the hieratic foundations of social order. Worse, it prevented the state from claiming sacral authority—and a state without absolute spiritual sovereignty, Evola argued, is no state at all.[45] At the root of the Christian schism is its belief in a transcendent God. Its "dualistic mythology," Evola charged, simultaneously makes human beings too servile (before God) and too rebellious (before human authorities). And this was something Christianity inherited largely from Judaism. Evola professed not to be an anti-Semite, merely a spiritual enemy of biblical monotheism. Yet he undeniably contributed to it, writing an introduction to a 1937 edition of *The Protocols of the Elders of Zion,* where he claimed that the forgery should not be "ignored or dismissed." For Evola, the *Protocols* were literally false but figuratively true. There was no Jewish cabal directing world events, but there was an "occult war" between Tradition and its powerful, if hidden, enemies. Evola warned of "cultural bolshevism," the ideological discrediting "of authority, of tradition, of race, or of fatherland," and he left little doubt that its root is the biblical teaching of human equality. It was the ongoing tragedy of Western history that Christianity did more than universalize Jewish values among the gentiles – it built social structures, both secular and religious, that prevented the return of Tradition.[46]

Violence and Utopia

At the time of his death in 1974, Evola was the most influential intellectual on the European radical right. In Italy he was associated with Ordine Nuovo and Avanguardia Nazionale, extra-parliamentary groups who sought a radical confrontation with the Italian state. Their use of Evola's texts in magazines, manuals, and training sessions was well known, and Evola praised them for their fidelity to illiberal principles, despite their ties to neo-Nazi parties. Some of their members would be convicted of bombings and involvement in a series of failed coups in the 1960s and 1970s. As he had done in a courtroom decades earlier, Evola again denied moral complicity, arguing that his teachings were not even his own, since they had a primordial origin, beyond individual human discovery. But from his apartment on the Corso Vittorio Emanuele II, he continued to mentor new disciples. He was "our Marcuse, only better," one student recalled.[47]

In recent decades, Evola has continued to attract new readers, first in France, where translations of his writings promoted a revival in paganism, and later in Russia, Eastern Europe, and, most recently, the United States, where radicals find a bracing attack on the legitimacy of liberal elites. They find in Evola a remarkable imaginative capacity to think about the world from beyond the boundaries liberalism has assigned it. What human life has been, is, might be, and should be – Evola offered the most comprehensive expression of anti-democratic, anti-liberal, anti-egalitarian, and anti-Christian principles in the twentieth century. To read him is to journey through a fantastic world of mythology, esotericism, mysticism, and pseudo-ethnology.[48] But his thought, for all its eccentricity, also reflected the intellectual traditions he detested most. In dreaming of building the ideal state and constructing a new man, he echoed the perennial utopian theme: once upon a time there was a perfect state, until a moral catastrophe destroyed it.

Evola imagined that such a state once existed and would exist again, when the wheel of history returned to the world of Tradition. Yet the world he imagined broke with the utopian tradition in Western thought and literature as well. Evola did not dream of a perfected state in which human life would be free from insecurity, violence, greed, misery, competition, and want. He did not hope to end pain and danger, to unite men in bonds of love, or to reconcile freedom and equality. Evola's fantasy was not of the mighty laid low and the humble raised up. It offered something more beguiling and arguably more necessary to those who, like him, experience modernity as a time of spiritual dispossession, and who fear irrelevance more than exploitation. Evola dreamed of a world of absolutely fixed and certain meanings, where human identities, in all their forms, bore the indelible chrism of sacred destiny. He fantasized about a world saturated with meanings so thick, so absolute, and so unchallengeable that they could create reflections of eternity in time. Evola did not live in hopeful anticipation of a better world after this one – the dream of heaven he called a "hallucination." He wished for a world after liberalism where holiness was again experienced in the otherwise cruel necessities of today. Both Christianity and liberalism teach us to see such necessities as things to be reformed and in need of redemption. But for those who prefer to see them as charged with the highest spiritual meaning, Evola's dream can tell them why.

Chapter 3

THE ANTI-SEMITE

Francis Parker Yockey played dangerous games. He sought out moments of extreme peril—"boundary situations," as philosophers call them—whose high stakes could prove the strength and sincerity of his commitments. His search did not lead him to foxholes or mountainsides. It took him into the unmapped world of the fascist underground, to places where identities were often concealed, borders frequently ignored, and loyalties rarely clear. He tested the purity of his devotion to what he called the Idea, undertaking the lonely sacrifices and voluntary risks that he believed its defense required. But in the end, it was not the games that he played with radical regimes and their proxies that did him in. It was not his espionage in the Soviet bloc, his propaganda campaigns in the Middle East, his work in Cuba, or his outlaw organizing in Germany. It was lost luggage.

When American Airlines flight 47 arrived in San Francisco on the evening of June 3, 1960, the passenger calling himself "Richard Hatch" had no premonition of the disaster about to ensnare him. He had stayed a step ahead of the FBI and State Department for a decade, traveling through four continents on forged papers, but a delayed flight made this his last destination. His inability to claim his luggage in Fort Worth, following a hurried connection, proved costly when airline employees attempted to discern its owner. What they discovered after opening the luggage would set tabloids buzzing. It was not the absence of clues as to the owner's identity. It was the bizarre surplus of them. Who was the well-dressed man appearing, under different names, in American, German, British, and Canadian passports? And which of the seven birth certificates was his, if any? The contents of the gray Samsonite suitcase only heightened the mystery—a typewriter, an address book written in code, German translations of Baroque Spanish literature, and drafts of three pornographic short stories. Confused and alarmed, the airline contacted the FBI, which judged that one name sounded suspiciously like that of a man they had been monitoring since 1939.

Yockey's arrest five days later in an Oakland apartment, following a thwarted escape attempt, marked the end of a long-running search by law enforcement and the beginning of a media frenzy. The time was ripe for a story of false identities and international intrigue. In the preceding weeks, Adolph Eichmann had been captured in Argentina by Mossad, an American U-2 spy plane had been shot down over Soviet territory, and the American Nazi Party had been launched by George Lincoln Rockwell. As the details of Yockey's case began to emerge, Bay Area papers ran daily updates on the "mystery man" charged with passport violation and held on a $50,000 bond. He was described as a fascist writer with declared Nazi sympathies, who, it was rumored, had collaborated with Communist governments in Europe and Latin America. The FBI told the press that his file was "loaded with dynamite" and the Anti-Defamation League named him as "the most important figure in world fascism we now know." If tabloid descriptions were to be believed, the San Francisco city jail was holding a prisoner equal parts James Bond and Che Guevara.[1]

As quickly as the story grew, however, it collapsed. Yockey was found dead in his cell on the morning of June 16 from apparent suicide. The U.S. commissioner hearing his case had requested a psychiatric examination of the forty-two-year-old defendant, and Yockey worried the questioning of his sanity meant he could not use the trial to defend himself or publicize his views. Fearing both institutionalization and the revelation of his web of associates, he took a lethal dose of potassium cyanide, leaving only a cryptic note about his hidden helpers. Yockey's story might have been forgotten had he not been visited just days before his death by one of the tiny number Americans who had read his work. Willis Carto would later build a network of right-wing organizations, including the influential Liberty Lobby, but his most important legacy was to have saved Yockey's writings from oblivion. He did more than secure publishing rights to his idol's work, which had been virtually unprocurable except in the form of mimeographs. He wrapped Yockey's life in a hagiography. In Carto's account, Yockey was not prosecuted for passport violations or illegal lobbying on behalf of foreign governments. He was a martyr—hunted, persecuted, and possibly killed by the very forces he expended his life in fighting.[2]

Today Yockey remains an object of special veneration on the American far right. Annual meetings are held in his name, where the story of his daring life and defiant last days is retold. You can even purchase a T-shirt bearing his image. Yockey is important, however, for reasons beyond his status as a cult figure. He is arguably America's preeminent fascist theorist, despite languishing in near complete intellectual obscurity. It almost beggars belief that

Yockey, whose writings have been translated into every major Western language, has never been the subject of an academic monograph. Perhaps he deserves to be forgotten as an extremist who wrote hateful words, defended indefensible actions, and associated with the worst of humanity. But if he is guilty of bigotry and worse, Yockey is innocent of shallowness. His revisionist history of the twentieth century, his phantom war against what is now called "cultural Marxism," and his anticipation of a resurgent Russia helping to correct a decadent West—the bizarre timeliness of his ideas, however unsavory their formulation, threatens to make Yockey the author of the future that he always insisted he was, even in his dying moments.

Imperium

Yockey came of age politically during the 1930s in Chicago, where he participated in the street activism of the German-American Bund and the Silver Shirts, an anti-Semitic organization modeled on paramilitary groups in Germany (and memorable chiefly for their striking blue-and-silver uniforms). He was no barstool fascist, however, looking for a fight with union heavies. Yockey was the youngest child of an upper-middle-class Catholic family, whose father had been a successful stockbroker before the Depression. Yockey always described himself as an artist, and nearly every recollection of him praised his gifts as a pianist. He studied at Georgetown University's School of Foreign Service before receiving a law degree, with honors, from the University of Notre Dame in 1941. His conversion to far-right politics, and his break with Marxism, occurred while reading Oswald Spengler's *The Decline of the West* during a school holiday.[3]

Yockey began his career as a lawyer and quickly became an assistant district attorney in Michigan. His undergraduate studies at Georgetown, his experience as a prosecutor, and his near-fluency in German enabled him to join the War Department as a civilian employee in 1945. He was assigned to the War Crimes Tribunal in Wiesbaden, tasked with helping prepare trial briefs and handling the clemency petitions of second-tier war criminals. His 1,600-page FBI file records the range of impressions that he left throughout his adult life. Described as affable and interesting by some, volatile and distant by others, he was universally regarded as brilliant and utterly derelict in performing his job. Yockey defended himself by claiming the tribunal was motivated by a desire for vengeance rather than justice, but it is impossible to credit his objectivity. He had other plans from the start. When he arrived in Germany in early 1946, he found the Thousand Year Reich prostrate—its cities in ruins, its leadership imprisoned or in hiding, its armed forces disbanded and disillusioned, and its people hungry, cold, and unemployed. Yockey had naively hoped to make contact with ideological resisters to the Allied occupation, but his failure to find them, at least in meaningful numbers, led him to rethink the nature of the war.

The experience inspired Yockey to write the book for which he is remembered. He left the continent after eleven months and traveled to Brittas Bay, Ireland, a remote hamlet on the Irish Sea. The thirty-year-old explained to friends that he sought the westernmost point of Europe from which to view the contemporary situation. In six months, without the aid of notes or a library, and drawing largely from memory, he produced the first two volumes of what his disciples later called "The Book." *Imperium* showed the signs of its hasty composition. It contained no footnotes, few quotations, and was written in a style that combined vatic pronouncement with dogmatic denunciation. Only 200 complete copies were printed, but it soon established its mysterious author as a major theorist on the dissident right. *Imperium* was printed in England under the pseudonym "Ulick Varange." "Ulick" is an Irish name, likely related to Ulysses, that means "reward of the mind." "Varange" referred to the Varangians, Norse mercenaries who assisted the early Russian state. The name suggested, then, a vision of Europe stretching from Ireland to the Urals, and an author who, though far from home, would fight for its unity.[4]

Imperium was a work of historical and philosophical revisionism. It offered an interpretation of events that Yockey acknowledged would sound absurd in 1950 but would be unassailable in 2050, he predicted. What had happened in the war? And who were its winners and losers? It did not make sense, he claimed, as a conventional military conflict. If the Western Allies had indeed prevailed, it was a strange victory that ultimately left them with less political power than they possessed at the start. Having entered the war to protect Central Europe, Yockey observed, they ended the war by relinquishing it. And as for their own empires, both the British and the French would see their possessions in Asia, India, and Africa begin to disintegrate almost overnight.[5] The war's conclusion saw the West in geopolitical retreat around the globe, led by an American regime whose outer show of strength masked deep ideological weaknesses. Yockey's history was eccentric, but his point was to show that its "surface events" concealed their true philosophical meaning.

Fundamentally, the war was not a military conflict at all, but an unresolved and continuing cultural struggle. At its heart was an antagonism between two possible futures for Western civilization. On one side were the allied ideologies of liberalism and communism. Though seemingly opposed, Yockey maintained, they shared many philosophical assumptions, especially about natural human equality, and differed only in the political implications they drew from them. Yockey predicted that their growing convergence, over the course of the coming Cold War, would reveal their ideological kinship. On the other side was the heroic, if flawed, attempt to build a society that could escape the slavery of communism and the anomie of liberalism. What was called fascism was merely a "provisional" response to a genuine social crisis. The 700 pages of *Imperium* made no explicit reference to national socialism or to Hitler, and its only mention of the Holocaust was to express doubt about the reported number of Jewish lives it claimed. Yockey's silences were morally obscene, but they were an essential part of his revisionism, which sought to change the focus from concrete historical events to what he called their higher meaning.[6]

The war did nothing to solve, and everything to exacerbate, what Yockey took to be the central dilemma of his time. How can a culture, after the wounding experiences of modernity, continue to give confident expression to itself? How can the West move from habitual self-criticism, and even occasional self-intolerance, to creative self-assertion? Yockey chose the word "imperialism" to describe his vision. It was the "Idea," as he put it, that captured the essence and destiny of the peoples of Europe and North America.[7] The first volume of *Imperium* reads like an ideological field manual. It is divided into short chapters, covering standard philosophical topics, that outline the basic logic of authoritarianism. At first glance, its doctrine appears unoriginal.[8] Politically, the ideal state is authoritarian, basing its legitimacy on submission to authority, rather than popular consent. "The source of government is the inequality of men," Yockey wrote.[9] Economically, this regime is socialist, subordinating the "rule of money" and all economic production to the state. Juridically, it places the rule of law under sovereign power, rather than constitutional procedures or a party system.

Imperium received a significant boost from a positive review by Julius Evola, who admired its attack on the fiction of the "neutral" and "pluralist" state. Evola gently criticized the book for having an unrealistic view of political realities, but he shared Yockey's horror at a world without rulers and ruled, and of human lives that aimed nothing higher than self-preservation and happiness.[10] Though the review helped to launch Yockey's career, its focus on practical politics failed to grasp the book's originality and the source of its lasting influence. *Imperium* argued that fascism, even in its most reflective forms, had been fundamentally misconceived, and that there was little purpose in preserving its conventional ideological structures. Its mistake was its narrow fixation with both nationalism and race, errors that led it to misidentify the West's "inner enemies," who now ruled over its societies. Yockey countered that politics is not a matter of biology or economics, and certainly not of morality or democratic elections. It is an expression of culture—and the uniquely Western compulsion to dominate every sphere of human life and thought.

Cultural Vitalism and Western Supremacy

Yockey was profoundly inspired by Spengler, whose historical imagination and speculative style freed him to rethink the nature of human society for himself. Yockey agreed that cultures are the unique bearers of an "idea" and that their histories could be understood only by grasping the "inner compulsion" through which they unfold.[11] He largely rejected, however, Spengler's understanding of what those prime symbols were, as well as his fatalism about their limited lifespans. Where Spengler saw the West as marked by individual striving for infinity, Yockey saw it as marked by the drive for group dominance. The idea of an imperium – the dream of universal dominion – was not a past episode in the political history of the West. It animated its life, thought, and art from its birth to the present. The purpose of Western civilization is "the subjection of the known world to its domination."[12] Yockey affirmed the political implications of this, and he defended, as we will see, the suppression of non-Western peoples and ideas within Western nations. But his deepest interests, as well as his darkest fears, were in the realm of cultural activity.

Yockey called his theory "cultural vitalism," and its elaboration filled the second volume of *Imperium*. He boasted that it would eventually become an academic discipline in its own right, forming the key to all social interpretation in the twenty-first century. *Vitalism* was a term connected with European philosophers reacting against scientific naturalism, and Yockey showed an awareness of their arguments, which he put to his own purposes. He argued that human beings are distinguished from animals in virtue of their capacity to risk their lives for something beyond life itself. To live as a human being is to be one who "puts something else before his own life and security."[13] In its most primal manifestation, this capacity is expressed in a physical struggle for prestige, in a competition for honor rather than material goods. But for Yockey there was a higher and purer expression of this human striving for preeminence. It is found in cultural and artistic creation, in which human beings impose lasting form on a domain of human life.[14]

Yockey believed that human life could be understood only through the thoughts and deeds of exceptional men. In explaining this, his primary guide was Thomas Carlyle, the nineteenth-century founder of the "great man" school of history, who is mentioned sixteen times in *Imperium*. From Carlyle, Yockey learned to read the history of culture as the biography of outstanding individuals. Human history is the record of great men giving form and life to a culture. Yockey's sociology of knowledge was a kind of heroic Platonism. It imagined that artistic, theoretical, and political "geniuses," as he called them, impart their ideas to the mass of humanity, whose lives are ennobled, indeed elevated out of animality, by their participation in human greatness. Yockey made reference to canonical figures in music, painting, philosophy, and science, whose contributions were so important as to have permanently changed their fields, and to have given rise to traditions of thought that carry their legacies. But his genealogies, and the philosophical basis he claimed for them, were of secondary concern. Yockey's goal was to show that the titans of Western culture had all been inwardly driven by the same idea—the ambition to rule souls.

The West is an imperial culture. The idea of "world-domination" is the spiritual basis and goal of all its achievements. Yockey did not mean, and in fact strenuously denied, that its culture serves to reinforce and justify the material interests of its ruling classes. That would be to say that what is seemingly "higher" in human life is merely an ideological reflection of what is "lower." Yockey saw the relation the other way around—it is not culture that follows power, but politics that follows culture. He argued that Western culture, in all its modes and styles, has an innately and uniquely aristocratic mission. It aims at being regarded as universally normative—as embodying the highest standards of excellence, truth, or beauty. The prestige that it seeks, in other words, is simply the universal recognition of its own supremacy. Yockey therefore read the history of

Western civilization as the story of its insuppressible drive to see its ideas, values, laws, styles, and institutions triumph over others. While the activities of philosophers, missionaries, scientists, artists, and statesmen might look different, Yockey maintained, they were all motivated by the imperial dream to dominate rival ways of life and thought.[15]

Yockey's "vitalism" made reference to Plato, Aquinas, Dante, Copernicus, Shakespeare, Rembrandt, and Napoleon. If the references were never explained, the message was unmistakable. To be true to its identity, to be in continuity with its own nature, the West must regard itself as the preeminent culture, as the "master" civilization. Yockey did not account for the metaphysical origin of this "idea," nor did he explain how it differed essentially from those of other cultures. But he argued that it laid on the peoples of Europe and North America a special burden, rather than a simple right to privilege. Yockey wrote in a tone more anguished than triumphal, and *Imperium* often sweated with unease. He worried that Western identity was so bound up with a belief in its superiority, so dependent upon its perceived preeminence, that it would cease to survive if it came to believe otherwise. It would be spiritually lethal, shattering to its self-image, to see itself as a mere equal in the community of world cultures. Yockey professed to be a pagan and a polytheist, but his theory of Western identity borrowed from his Catholic upbringing and education. He insisted that the existence of the West depended entirely upon the strength of its common "faith." Not its faith in the biblical God, which he rejected, but a belief in its own supremacy.

As Yockey surveyed Western nations after the war, however, he perceived a disturbing change in their leadership classes. He claimed the West had historically been led by men who understood its civilizational soul, or at least took counsel from those who did. He called them its "cultural stratum" and invoked them as a kind of invisible empire that linked ruling elites across national boundaries and historical periods.[16] He imagined them as the guardians of a shared patrimony and the intellectual field generals of a common mission. They were in the schools of Charlemagne, the villas of the Medici, the courts of French and Spanish kings, and the classrooms of German gymnasia. Though they were not a hereditary elite, they formed the basis of a caste system. Crucially, they shielded imperial ideals from egalitarian hostilities, upholding the fundamental importance of rank and distinction among human beings. But today, Yockey complained, a very different elite has come to shape the minds of the liberal West. And its goal is not the defense of its indigenous culture, but its democratic demotion and debasement. In place of a culture of heroism, the elite have imposed a culture of critique, whose goal is not only to redistribute cultural power more equally; it is to protect an alien people, whose ideas have secretly distorted their host culture.

Cultural Marxism and the Jewish Century

Yockey had his eye on the future and his goal in *Imperium* was the fundamental reorientation of the American and European hard right. He counseled it to set aside the national rivalries and petty disagreements that had divided it in the past and to unite around a shared imperial identity. He initially asked Oswald Mosley to publish the book under his own name, believing the former head of the British Union of Fascists could draw a wide readership.[17] But *Imperium* found an audience on its own and quickly became a doctrinal inspiration for an emerging fascist international. At first glance it seemed to encourage new thinking. "The attempt to interpret history in terms of race must be abandoned," Yockey announced, calling it "grotesque" to believe that races could be ranked or measured. Yockey even argued that it had been a strength of Western culture, since the late Roman era, to have welcomed "strong minorities" into its common life. "The race one feels is everything, the anatomic-geographic group to which one belongs means nothing."[18]

But there were limits to assimilation, and *Imperium* also sought to rekindle some of the deadliest ideas of the 1930s for the coming multicultural world. Yockey warned that the Soviet occupation of European lands was not nearly as dangerous as the ideological occupation of Western minds. He asked why Americans and Europeans felt increasingly hesitant, even guilty, about asserting their group identity and interests. His answer was that they suffered from "culture distortion," a condition in which a people contracts ideas and values that it fails to realize are self-harming.[19] Who were the "inner enemies" responsible for it? Yockey's frame of reference was mid-century America, a nation whose history as a European "colony" left it especially vulnerable to distortion. He discussed African Americans at length, but judged that they were culturally "parasitic" and lacked the creative capacity to pose genuine dangers.[20] His concern was with another minority, who had lived inside the West for a millennium, storing up resentment at its achievements and preparing a theoretical attack on its self-understanding.

Yockey was an anti-Semite of a particularly virulent and innovative kind. The signs were evident already in his early speaking and writing, which drew FBI attention while he was still in his twenties. But Yockey had also concluded that racial anti-Semitism, and the reductive mentality it encouraged, had led to tragic consequences. Not so much for murdered Jews, for whom he showed little concern, but for those unaware of their insidious menace. He thus undertook to reveal the true threat, hidden even from hardened anti-Semites, posed by Jews and Jewish ideas. His primary fear was not that Jews had seized control of political institutions or manipulated the invisible levers of economic power. Yockey attempted to turn vulgar anti-Semitism on its head and to refine its explanatory power. His deepest worry was not that Westerners might be exploited by Jews. It was that they might unwittingly *become* Jews. There indeed *was* a Jewish conspiracy at work in the modern world. It took place on a metaphysical plane, he asserted, and yet had little to do with the religious practice of Judaism.

Yockey identified the Jewish spirit with a certain strain of post-Enlightenment rationality. Its distinguishing mark was a mentality of suspicion, and its message spread wherever critical rationality punctured the pretentions of European life. Its most powerful expression was found in the theories of Marx and Freud, and Yockey devoted considerable time to analyzing their intellectual legacies.[21] He identified them as the most destructive of all assaults on Western culture, since they used the tools of Western rationality to strike at its very soul. They did so by unmasking appearances—by showing that behind the impressive façade of Western life hid deeply unflattering truths. Its artistic and political traditions were not the expression of a unique aspiration for beauty and excellence. They were products of the most common drives for mammon and sex. Yockey believed that these ideas, and their countless insinuations in entertainment and education, did more than undermine the self-conception of Western peoples. They aimed at nothing less than "the animalization of Culture-man."[22]

Yockey's anti-Semitism borrowed tropes from Christian history—that Jews are legalistic, fleshly, and unbelieving—and recoded them into modern, secular terms. Jews became a people defined by their materialism, skepticism, and reliance on critical theory, and to adopt this mentality was, for Yockey, to see the world in Jewish terms – indeed, to become effectively Jewish. Yockey's own life was anything but traditional (his FBI file records his compulsive use of prostitutes and even his work as a gigolo), yet he accused Jews of fomenting social decadence.[23] Family breakdown, blurred gender roles, degrading popular music, rampant consumerism, and the all-round rise of social deviancy – all were attributed to Jewish ideas that served to liberate human desires from social control. In Yockey's phantasmagoria, the Jews were simply everywhere in modern life, lurking behind both capitalism and communism, cosmopolitanism and nationalism, higher education and mass entertainment.

Yockey therefore saw the twentieth century as the long-awaited time and place of the Jews' metaphysical revenge on their host culture. It was *rationality* that Jews had distorted. No longer a power for commanding reality, it had become a critical faculty grounded in our shared frailty. It turned its users from deference toward heroes and encouraged suspicion about inequalities; away from respect for high culture, towards a fascination with triviality. Yockey acknowledged that the entry of Jews into modern life had been preceded by democratic and economic revolutions (for which he blamed the Protestant Reformation). But once safely inside the West, Jews set out on "a mission of revenge and destruction."[24] To what end? Yockey's anti-Semitism was motivated by paranoid envy. The ideas of Marx and Freud were part of a group survival strategy that merely extended, under secular disguise, Judaism's practices of critical reasoning. And having persuaded the West to become an open society, the Jew had retained his closed world – encouraging skepticism and tolerance among others, while "keeping his own phylacteries."[25]

Yockey's arguments were crude, but they helped to establish an influential discourse about what later came to be called "cultural Marxism." It claims that there is an intellectual movement, rooted in radical European thought, whose purpose is to dismantle Western culture through the remorseless application of critical theory. A prominent advocate has defined it as a "a theory of criticizing everyone and everything everywhere," an "infinite and unending criticism of the status quo."[26] The notion of "cultural Marxism" has been ridiculed by scholars, who mock its conspiratorial story of émigré scholars infiltrating American universities. But in the minds of believers, it describes a prominent feature of our public life. To them "cultural Marxism" is the massively influential project of redistributing cultural power and representation, especially as it intersects with differences of race, sex, and gender. Yockey was one of the first to fabricate a counterdiscourse to it, one that identified its ideals not as part of the rich legacy of Western self-criticism, but as lethal to its very existence. By the late 1960s, his ideas (and image) would be invoked by campus activists claiming that tenured disciples of Marx and Freud were destroying American culture. They would not be the last.[27]

Ex Oriente Lux

Yockey popularized his arguments in *The Proclamation of London* and *The Enemy of Europe,* slim volumes that aimed at making his larger work more accessible.[28] But his output declined sharply after 1952, when he felt pressured by law enforcement to go underground. His activities over the next eight years, now a part of far-right lore, are difficult to chronicle in detail. Because the State Department sought to revoke his passport and the FBI wanted him for questioning—Yockey was the subject of multiple memos by J. Edgar Hoover—he lived and traveled under a bewildering number of aliases. He relied on a small group of American and European patrons for housing and financial support, both of which were desperately needed by an activist who often lived in hostels and went without meals. Yet through FBI informants and the recollection of friends, the general itinerary of his remaining years can be known.

Sometime in the early 1950s, Yockey left for the Middle East, where he joined an Egyptian ministry that produced anti-Semitic propaganda. We know little about his activities, save that he met future Egyptian president Gamal Abdel Nasser. Nothing that he wrote at that time has been discovered, but he likely worked alongside former Nazis who found employment in defense and intelligence programs in the region after the war (some of whom converted to Islam and took Muslim names).[29] Yockey did not remain in Egypt for long, however, and he soon turned to the Communist East. In November 1952, fourteen Jewish members of the Communist Party of Czechoslovakia, including its former general secretary, were put on trial for treason and espionage. Stalin had orchestrated the show trial as part of his extensive purge of Jewish intelligentsia and party leaders in the wake of Israel's alignment with the United States. Yockey watched the trial from a courtroom gallery, and it inspired one of the most important writings of the postwar radical right.[30]

Yockey's article was titled "What Is Behind the Hanging of the Eleven Jews in Prague?" It hailed the event as a turning-point in modern history. Yockey often wrote about the hidden meaning of political events, and in his imagination, the trial communicated a clear signal to dissident factions in the West. Its message was that the Kremlin had turned against culture distortion and had repudiated Jewish ideology. The executions were evidence that Russian nationalists had wrestled control of the regime from Jewish Bolsheviks, spelling the eventual end of the Marxist state and its return to a traditional Russian regime. Yockey's article, written during the height of the Red Scare, baffled even some of his followers. It claimed the Soviet Union was no longer a serious ideological threat to the West, a fact that required a complete realignment of rightist thinking. "Henceforth, all must perforce reorient their policy in view of the undeniable reshaping of the world-situation."[31]

Yockey's article was circulated in small magazines throughout Europe, the Middle East, and the Americas. Its reverberations did not go unnoticed. It was published in a climate of mounting panic about covert Soviet support for Western groups promoting neutrality in the Cold War. An alarmed *Washington Post* article identified "Ulich Varange" as the intellectual architect of a brewing red-brown alliance in Europe. A national magazine story similarly referred to Yockey as the "mastermind" behind a revival of far-right sympathy for West German nonalignment. Such worries were unfounded—even Yockey had little hope for an immediate fascist revival in Europe—but the FBI had grown more concerned as well. A 1954 memo records that Yockey was "engaged in fascist activities on an international scale" and "had declared that his main goal is to unite all fascists in the world" against the United States. (The FBI did not know that Yockey had also been contacted by Sen. Joseph McCarthy to draft a speech about American double-standards toward Russia.)[32]

Yockey's analysis was quickly contradicted by events, but its reading of Soviet policy was less important for what it predicted than for what it portended. As scholars and analysts have recently begun to notice, it marked the beginning of a rethinking about

Russia on the radical right whose distant echoes are heard today.[33] Yockey saw the Prague trial as a sign that the Soviet revolution had failed to destroy traditional Russian identity, and that its native culture, undistorted by modern thinking, would rise to challenge the decadent West. His ideas built on the work of German thinkers who had earlier envisioned a postliberal alliance with Russia, as well as the short-lived ideology of "national Bolshevism" and its attempted synthesis of communism and nationalism. Yockey closely studied these thinkers while at Georgetown, where he was introduced to early "Eurasianists" who argued that control of the Eurasian heartland was the key to geopolitical dominance in Europe.

Yockey did not believe Russian culture was essentially or even potentially Western. In fact, just the opposite. Russia "detests Western culture, civilization, nation, arts, state-forms, ideas, religions, cities, and technology," he wrote in *Imperium*.[34] But he also believed that the destinies of Russia and the West were historically intertwined, and that their differences could be salutary, rather than destructive, for the West. He therefore sought to clear the theoretical ground for a "symbiosis" between them.[35] At the heart of his thinking was the assumption that "true Russia," as he called it, is primitive, mystical, and communal. Its cultural soul is therefore innately opposed to individualism, rationalism, and materialism, as evidenced by its supposed rejection of Marxism. Russia preserved everything the liberal West had squandered. Where the West had grown tired, divided, effeminate, and self-critical, Russia had remained vigorous, tribal, masculine, and self-protective. Yockey acknowledged that Russia still threatened the West militarily, and he did not discount the possibility of an invasion. But the mere threat of occupation, as well as Russia's ferocious opposition to liberalism, he speculated, could serve to correct a wayward West.

Between 1955 and 1958 Yockey dropped off the map. He published nothing and avoided detection from law enforcement. According to confidants, he went to work for Communist governments in Central Europe and Latin America. Yockey was undergoing an intellectual transformation that would shape his legacy, but he had not become a Marxist. He had become an avowed enemy of an American regime that had betrayed its founding ""individual imperialism" and had chosen to spread the "ethical syphilis" of liberal culture in a global Cold War. It was to counteract its spreading influence that he apparently chose to collaborate with East German and Czech intelligence services, likely working as a courier. Rarely in any location for long, Yockey also lived in Cuba, where he was employed at a magazine and established contacts with the Cuban military. As the Second World War receded into the past, Yockey became more sympathetic toward Third World movements and more despondent about American culture. And when he reappeared in California in the late 1950s, he would find his worst fears confirmed and his days numbered.[36]

A World in Flames

Yockey spent most of his last years drifting up and down the West Coast. He worked at odd jobs, dabbled in amateur pornography, and leached off a string of older women. He said he felt like a stranger in America, a land whose pollution by commerce and critique had robbed it of seriousness. America was a land where "every day is a birthday," a place that left no room for great souls or great sacrifices.[37] And its openness, he complained, had rendered it culturally sterile. Americans increasingly read the books that outsiders wrote about them, watched the movies that outsiders produced for them, and debated the ideas that outsiders permitted them. After a decade of underground work, Yockey seemed to sense the end of his apostolate. But he was not without hope, and in the anti-colonial movements blossoming around the globe, he found reason to believe that a clarifying moment of danger, long awaited, might at last be near.

In January 1960, while living in San Francisco, he finished his last essay. "The World in Flames" was a meditation on the course of history after 1945 and an acknowledgment of the Beatniks as the inspiration for a younger generation.[38] But Yockey saw raw possibilities in the counterculture, and his opening to it would influence, as we will see next, a philosopher who has been called his "intellectual successor."[39] Yockey envisioned a multipolar world and its teeming "pluriverse" of values. For the first time in centuries, the West would confront a world that it did not, for the most part, make or govern. Yockey predicted the rising of the world's young peripheries against its aging center. He noted his pleasure in a new generation of leaders in Indonesia, Pakistan, India, Ghana, Yugoslavia, and Sudan that marked a "growing tide of neutralism." Yockey's prose, formerly lawyerly and disciplined, was now apocalyptic and emotional. He pondered the outbreak of a Third World War and fantasized that it might put an end to a senescent West that had lost its desire to fight, reproduce, and defend itself against adversaries.[40] He had six months to live.

When he met Willis Carto just days before his death, Yockey spoke about fantastic escape plans and complained about being jailed with nonwhites. But Carto, peering through the chicken wire that separated them, realized he had an opportunity to become the keeper of a legend. For generations of readers, Carto's hagiographic introductions to *Imperium* gave the American far right something it never had: a prisoner of conscience, whose only crime was to have written a book. In the decade that followed, Carto became a major agitator in right-wing politics, specializing in the ideological harassment of mainstream conservatives. He wrapped his work in the story and iconography of its martyred saint, distributing Yockey's book to his network of campus activists. *Imperium* cannot be read for recreation or for pleasure, and it is impossible to think that many students read it. But Carto understood that it did not matter, since its ideas were haloed by the witness of Yockey's life.[41]

If it is easy for us to reject Yockey's ideas, it is more difficult to judge his life. It is hard to refuse any admiration to those who not only decline the comforts of life, but risk death in the pursuit of an ideal. Of course, in the case of terrorists or gang members we do just that. But the man who seeks out self-sacrifice, rather than self-preservation, the man who denies his material well-being for the sake of a mere symbol – such a man is still the enduring problem of liberalism. Liberalism calculates that our desire to fight over abstract symbols can be overcome, or at least channeled into more productive pursuits. But there will always be men and women who cannot be satisfied this way, and who believe that a culture without life-or-death causes will revolve around empty pleasures and diversion. Say what you will about Yockey, he *starved* for his Idea. His vow was to "risk all and die for an Idea," and did he not? Against this ugly fact it is somehow not enough to say his work is speculatively dubious, morally grotesque, and historically simplistic. For it is above all deadly sincere, his words having been sealed by the testimony of his life. And for those who turn to his writings, there is a clarity and zeal for a cause that are undeniable, even when the cause is revolting. Yockey's personal papers record his profound sense of mission in life and his intense belief that his destiny was to be denied all earthly pleasure and happiness. He believed that he was fated to live and die for dangerous truths. Yockey cannot be refuted without being understood, as both a thinker and as a man. We should read and ponder Yockey, not to render his hateful causes less hateful, but only so that we can understand those who also say, "I believe in the lonely agonies of superior men."[42]

Chapter 4

THE PAGAN

As he watched the first barricades going up in Paris's Latin Quarter in May 1968, Alain de Benoist might have been mistaken for a student protester. A university dropout and self-described flâneur, he spent his days reading radical journals and visiting left-wing bookshops. Though he had lived comfortably in Paris since childhood and was a product of its most elite schools, he welcomed the upheaval that plunged France into a national crisis. "I loved the electric atmosphere of the demonstrations and the movement of the crowds," he later recalled, "the clashes with the police, the smell of tear gas." Benoist was reading Sartre, and siding with the Maoists against the Trotskyists, but he was no man of the left, and his admiration for the protesters concealed a different cast of mind.[1]

At twenty-five years old, Benoist was already a veteran of the French far right, having spent six years as a leader of the Federation of Nationalist Students and as a contributor to magazines with ideological roots in Vichy. If his reading habits leaned toward the revolutionary left, his writing placed him squarely on the ultranationalist right. Benoist was known as the author of revanchist tracts on French Algeria and Rhodesia, as well as for his collaboration with prominent French fascists, associations that would cloud his reputation in decades to come. He had also published articles in American magazines founded by disciples of Francis Parker Yockey, where he expressed sympathy for racial segregation.[2] Benoist's involvement in political organizing dated to his teenage years, but a recent intellectual conversion, inspired by a study of ancient philosophy, had led him to reassess his work and to see politics in a new light.

The May demonstrations confirmed his intuition about the changing nature of French politics—an intuition, you might say, about the link between the bookstores and the boulevards. Although the establishment right enjoyed electoral success in the Fifth Republic—the left would not win the presidency until 1981—Benoist believed the right had vanished as a serious presence in the nation's intellectual life. He complained of its bitterness and nostalgia, and lamented his own contributions to its flirtation with xenophobia.[3] By comparison, the New Left was everything the French right was not. Politically powerless, it pulsed with intellectual vitality and cultural creativity. Benoist sensed that the new social movements, focusing on women and minorities, had been advanced by cultural influence rather than political power.

While Benoist harbored deep disagreements with the New Left, he also thought its ideas and vocabulary, especially its concern for group identities, could be adapted to better purposes. Just days before the Paris protests, Benoist and a group of colleagues had gathered in Lyon to form what would now be called a think tank. It took the name "Research and Study Group for European Civilization," better known by its French acronym GRECE (French for "Greece"). Its goal was to create for the dissident right what journals, bookshops, and academic departments had provided the left—an intellectual community, removed from the cut and thrust of daily political exchange, that could influence the *longue durée* of French culture. The group came to be called the New Right, and its magazines and conferences attained notoriety in the late 1970s, when the founding of the National Front led alarmed journalists to see it as a Frankfurt School for reactionaries.[4]

The French New Right is now a minor presence in French political life, but its intellectual founder has never seemed more relevant. Today Benoist disavows his youthful views and claims to have transcended the conventional left-right divide. He is known for promoting the "right to difference," a principle that claims to defend the diversity of cultures and the identities that constitute them. While his writing over four decades has consistently bid for the respect of the academic left, Benoist remains anathema to it. He is the principal architect of "identitarianism," a social philosophy, influential in the European far right, that aims to protect cultures against their displacement by immigration and their distortion by abstract ideologies. Benoist rejects liberalism's holiest principle, and the religious faith on which it secretly rests. What makes political life possible is not discovering what we share in common. It is recognizing what permanently sets us apart.

Polytheism of Values

Alain de Benoist was born in 1943 to an upper-middle-class Catholic family with no political affiliations. From youth he considered himself a nonconformist and religious nonbeliever, and reports that his dream was to challenge popular opinion with ideas of his own. His efforts met with early success. In 1978, the French Academy awarded him a prestigious grand prize for a three-volume work entitled *View from the Right*. The volumes collected over 100 essays and reviews that he had published since becoming a journalist in his twenties. Benoist's ambition in founding GRECE was to cultivate new lines of academic inquiry from a rightist perspective. This never happened, but what he had in mind can be glimpsed in his early journalism.[5]

Benoist used his weekly columns to speculate on the origins of European identity, and to introduce heterodox ideas from philosophy and science. Essays on the Etruscans, Celts, Franks, Vikings, and Homeric Greeks signaled his willingness to seek political insight in unusual sources. His guiding idea, then as now, was that characteristically European attitudes and values exist, and can be found in the pre-Christian heritage of the West. Benoist had already written a small book on the Indo-Europeans, and he claimed these "first Europeans" as a cultural (and not simply linguistic) community that formed the common origin of the continent's life. "We want to rekindle the old spirit of European cultures," he explained in a 1979 interview.[6] His essays avoided partisan commentary, aiming instead to seed public discussion with controversial ideas and thinkers, especially those espousing inegalitarian or anti-Christian points of view (examples included racial theorist Arthur de Gobineau, biblical scholar Ernst Renan, and ethologist Konrad Lorenz).

His work struck many as eccentric. The French right was then divided between traditional Catholics, Gaullist nationalists, and Orléanist liberals. Benoist repudiated all three camps, gleefully and without apology. He announced that his values were illiberal, relativist, and pagan, and that he had no special reverence for Christianity, the nation-state, or capitalism. In what sense was Benoist on the right? His conservatism reflected an older sensibility, he argued, one that saw the heterogeneity of peoples as the "only true wealth of the world." He regarded its "diversity and inequalities" to be a good, and its "progressive homogenization" to be an evil.[7] Benoist's early essays were eclectic and bore a style that marks his writing to this day – impassioned, idiosyncratic, and pleading for scholarly legitimacy. But the work found a readership, and its author was soon interviewed by *Playboy* and asked about his political ambitions.

Benoist chose instead to commit himself to a "theoretical life," and his thinking began to deepen.[8] In a 1979 article, he attempted to explain the philosophical basis for his emerging worldview. It was a rare statement of first principles. The proper foundation of rightist thinking, he declared, is that of nominalism. Nominalism is a metaphysical doctrine, originating in late medieval theology, that denied the real existence of universals. It held that only particular beings or objects exist, and that universals are merely conventional names (*nomina*) invented by the mind. Because nominalism denies reason's ability to know universal truths or natures, it is often accused by conservatives of undermining natural order and denying a common good. Benoist stood such arguments on their head. Only nominalism, he maintained, can defend traditional ways of life and values such as excellence, heroism, and honor.

Benoist was uninterested in abstract arguments for or against nominalism, which he subtly turned into a theory of group differences. Nominalism is true to an experience – an experience of the world as rich in human diversity, abundant in inequalities, and resistant to universal categories. To such a world, he suggested, we can take one of two possible attitudes. Nominalism respects, indeed venerates, the variety of human styles and forms, appreciating them in their particularity and uniqueness. Nominalism therefore reveres local traditions and loyalties, affirming that ideas are "real" only when "incarnated" in specific people and places.[9] What Benoist called "universalism" is a contrasting attitude. Its vision is not of the deep differences separating human beings, but of the deep unity connecting them. Universalism values similarities over differences, and unity over pluralism.

Benoist would develop these themes in later work, but his critique of universalism marked an important turn. It committed him to opposing all attempts to evaluate social identities in relation to a single norm or standard. In proposing a "polytheism of values," as he put it, Benoist hinted at something more than his embrace of pluralism, however. He was also avowing his paganism. Benoist professes to have never believed in God, having rejected theism as a child after pondering questions about freewill and divine omnipotence. When he was twenty-six, he participated in an infamous public debate at the Sorbonne with a Catholic graduate student named Jean-Luc Marion (now among France's most distinguished philosophers), in which Benoist argued that Christian values, even at their purest, had corrupted European civilization.[10] Yet Benoist has also consistently and credibly claimed to be a religious thinker. His 1981 book *On Being a Pagan* is among his most personal and most widely read, and claimed paganism as the most authentically European attitude toward life.

On Being a Pagan warned that the fate of Europe hung on a choice between two warring visions of human life: Christian monotheism and paganism. According to Benoist, pagan doctrine is simple: the world is holy and eternal, uncreated and imperishable. "Far from desacralizing the world," he wrote, "paganism sacralizes it in the literal sense of the word; it regards the world as sacred."[11] For paganism, the divine does not transcend the world. It exists in the powers and mysteries immanent to human experience. Benoist had experimented with neo-pagan rituals early in life, but he did not endorse building altars to Apollo or reviving worship of Odin. He defended paganism as an attitude about the terrestrial sources of human value, and hence about the nature of political community. Paganism roots all value – all meaning, inspiration, and fulfillment – in our communion with the natural and social worlds. It places human beings on a continuum with nature and the divine, seeing all existence as alive with the sacred. Paganism is therefore a humanism. It recognizes human beings, in their social nature, as the source of the gods, who "exist" as models that we should strive to equal.

Christianity instead places the highest value in a transcendent realm, outside of humanity, which is universally valid for all people. Benoist alleged that Christianity thereby deforms our natural impulses and weakens our social relationships. We naturally respect and trust those like us, and avoid and distrust those who seem alien. We naturally admire beauty, health, and excellence, and pity the weak and ugly. But where paganism consecrates our vital instincts, seeing them as the healthy basis of social life, Christianity aims to reform them. It demands that we recognize the shared humanity and will the common good of all people, regardless of their condition or background. Benoist drew from controversial intellectual sources, but he did not openly defend cruelty or selfishness. He charged Christianity with an inability to recognize human differences as other than inessential or transitory. Its mistake is to deem people manifestly unequal in abilities, status, and character to be fundamentally the *same* – in virtue of possessing souls of equal dignity before God.[12]

Christianity therefore marked a rupture in human history, whose ongoing effects Benoist set himself to resisting. It began a process of "disembedding" human beings from rooted communities. Christianity revolutionized the social world – it gave human beings an individual identity apart from their family, homeland, and heritage. Benoist lamented that Christians imagine themselves as part of a universal community, one that welcomes no fewer than all people as potential members. Politics depends on the recognition of outsiders, yet the Christian church sees all people as potential members, indeed potential saints. "But if all men are brothers," Benoist countered, "then no one can truly be a brother."[13] *On Being a Pagan* sounded a political warning: Christianity, and the secular ideologies it birthed, cannot protect European peoples and cultures. Under its influence, Europe lives under a double occupation, existing under the power of a foreign religion and an alien deity. Benoist's remarkable conclusion was that the secular West and its emptying churches have never been more Christian. Its self-criticism, concern for victims, and fear of excluding outsiders estrange Europeans from the earthly homelands that he would next look to defend.

Folk Democracy

Benoist's work raised suspicions that he had not outgrown his early extremism, only camouflaged its expression, and he became a frequent target of the European press, appearing in literally hundreds of features in the late 1970s and early 1980s. He was often portrayed as a kind of "designer fascist," whose celebration of pagan values and human inequalities, though dressed in fashionable language, seemed all too reminiscent of a more grotesque ideology.[14] Even major journals in the United States, where his work was not yet available in translation, expressed concern over his rising stature. The criticisms had effect. Benoist lost his national newspaper column, and his profile in European intellectual life dimmed. But as his reputation moved toward the periphery, his work grew more focused.

In his 1985 book, *The Problem of Democracy,* Benoist responded to critics by examining the political regime that he believed was most consonant with European identity. If paganism was the most authentically European attitude toward life, democracy was its most authentic political form. From one perspective, the book was quaint. Benoist reproduced a standard account of the differences between ancient and modern democracy, highlighting their contrasting views of human liberty and equality. From another perspective, however, the book was prescient. It assembled an argument, increasingly popular among postliberals, about the deepest threat to popular sovereignty. Liberalism and democracy do not form a harmonious pair, Benoist claimed, but are in fact antithetical political programs, and their forced marriage threatens the very existence of self-governing peoples.[15]

Democracy is not the best of all possible regimes, nor is it a proper model for every developing society. Benoist rejected thinking about politics in universalist terms. Democracy is simply how the conscious practice of politics first and most influentially appeared in European history. Benoist turned to the democracy of ancient Greece as its paradigmatic instance. Its essential feature, he wrote, was its understanding of citizenship. In ancient democracy, to be a citizen was not to be an individual with rights and private interests of one's own. Nor did it presume membership in humanity as such. To be a citizen was to be a member of a particular people, with a defined territory and shared lineage, who exercise sovereignty over their political life. "Demos and ethnos coincide," he explained, and where there is no distinct "people," there can be no democracy.[16]

Benoist's description of ancient democracy drew on a venerable line of scholarship. It saw politics as a sphere of human freedom, transcending the concerns of the home, in which a people gave expression to its civic identity. Yet Benoist added controversial emphases of his own as well, and they revealed a vision of politics profoundly rooted in organic community. To be a member of a people, he insisted, is to share "a homeland and a history." It requires "cultural cohesion and a clear sense of shared heritage," enabling citizens to participate in a common "destiny." "Folk democracy," as he named this closed society, does not presume unanimity of opinion. But it does presuppose a relatively "homogenous" community, reflectively aware of its identity, to which its members feel bound by birth. Benoist left the character of this homogeneity ambiguous, saying only that a people must be animated by a "folk consciousness."[17]

Benoist admired ancient democracy not because he believed it could be recreated, but because it reflected a sound understanding of human identity, whose social contours he felt he was beginning to grasp. He drew on contemporary communitarian thinkers for support, arguing that human identity is always mediated through group memberships. Human beings do not exist, even in their most private aspects, as mere individuals, and it is a liberal illusion to imagine they do. They exist in "symbiosis" with their surrounding communities; with families that share an ancestral legacy; with nations that bestow civic membership; with spiritual and moral traditions that form character; and with cultures that initiate them into a pattern of life.[18] Benoist's language echoed themes in German romanticism, and he expressed a growing concern for preserving folk traditions in both the West and the Third World.[19] But his focus remained on contemporary Europe, which he believed suffered from a crisis of belonging.

"The profound cause of the crisis," he maintained, "is the unnatural alliance of democracy and liberalism."[20] Benoist is essentially an encyclopedist of anti-liberal ideas, and much of his writing consists of the diligent (and exhausting) cataloguing of arguments, drawn from across academic disciplines, that challenge liberal ideals. In his mind, liberalism is the ideological core of all Western societies, informing all its institutions and practices, and his rejection of it aims to be comprehensive. He traces its essential feature to its emphasis on individualism, which transfers sovereignty from the united "folk" to the autonomous individual. Liberal thinkers have characterized human nature in different ways, but Benoist claims they all agree the individual is the fundamental basis of political society. As an ideology, liberalism therefore places the individual before the group, and values personal freedom over social solidarity.[21]

Benoist is sometimes criticized for being unoriginal, and it is true that he rehearses long-standing critiques of liberalism. He charges that liberal theories are consistently contradicted by liberal realities. In theory, liberalism protects individuals from unjust authority, allowing them to pursue fulfilling lives apart from government coercion. In reality, it severs deep bonds of belonging, leaving isolated individuals exposed to, and dependent on, the power of the state. In theory, liberalism proposes a neutral vision of human nature, cleansed of historical residues and free of ideological distortions. In reality, it promotes a bourgeois view of life, placing a higher value on acquisition than virtue. In theory, liberalism makes politics more peaceful by focusing on the mundane rather than the metaphysical. In reality, it makes political life chaotic by splintering communities into rival factions and parties.[22]

The failings of liberalism are not accidental, in Benoist's opinion. They are a direct consequence of its central doctrine. In liberal ideology, individuals possess rights that are inherent to human nature and exist independent of political authority. Since these rights are prior to political life, they cannot be created or abolished by government. For the same reason, they are prior to duties, since all duties imply obligations to others (and there can be no duties where there are no others).[23] Benoist's claim, elaborated over dozens of books and repeated in hundreds of articles, is that the social logic of liberalism works to the evaporating of communal identity. His story is a familiar one. Relationships once rooted in a common heritage and history are redefined in terms of individual choice; values once embodied in a shared tradition become grounded in personal autonomy. What was organic has become voluntary – dependent on consent, motivated by self-interest, and possessing no lasting bond. And within such associations, Benoist laments, individuals retain their most cherished liberty, the freedom to withdraw their allegiance to it.

As confidence in liberalism crested in the 1990s, Benoist's views grew more contrarian. He argued that liberalism had rendered Europeans unable to act *as a people,* and he predicted that postliberal movements, rejecting the left-right divide, would soon challenge its dissolution of national identities. Liberalism claims that people should be free to choose their own path in life and that governments ought to protect and foster the exercise of this freedom. Benoist's accusation, paradoxical at first hearing, is that liberalism therefore regards all people as fundamentally *the same.* His writing returned to some of his earliest themes, now expressed in the tone of anti-globalism and the idiom of French postmodernism. He attacked what he called "Sameness," according to which human beings must be understood in reference to a single universal model. But human identities can be grounded neither in what we individually possess nor in what we universally share in common, he countered. They are founded instead in what sets our communities apart. Benoist had found his deepest philosophical footing, and his most controversial following.

Identity and Exclusion

In a 2000 book, *Manifesto for a European Renaissance,* Benoist called for the recovery of "clear and strong identities" as the basis of a post-liberal order.[24] Its arguments drew the admiration of movements on the radical right, who shared its concerns over immigration and multiculturalism. But Benoist's thinking had undergone a subtle transformation. As to what European identities are or ought to be, he was increasingly ambiguous. Benoist sometimes suggested that Europe is unique in having become philosophically aware of cultural pluralism, but he also cautioned that it possessed no unchanging essence across time, and that traditionalists were mistaken to believe it does.[25] Benoist is therefore a rightist but not, strictly speaking, a reactionary, since he does not believe a restoration of past social forms is possible or desirable. Modernity is irreversible, and its stripping of traditions and erasing of memories cannot not be simply overturned. It can, however, be overcome.

Benoist is a cultural revolutionary. His goal is to revive the ideological preconditions under which organic forms of European community might again take root after liberalism. "Meta-political" is how he describes his work, which focuses on shaping cultural attitudes and values rather than engaging in direct activism. "Metapolitics" places a higher value on theory than on policies or parties, believing that changes in cultural consciousness precede any social transformation ("We cannot have a Lenin without having had a Marx"[26]). Benoist's most important contribution to this metapolitical strategy is his philosophy of social identity. Its central thesis is that "man is an heir by nature," a being who experience meaning only through the extended self of inherited social memberships, rather than in what he experiences by himself.[27]

"Holism," as Benoist calls it, emphasizes that each human life is embedded in a social and cultural world, and that our "situatedness," far from being an impediment to self-realization, is what makes it possible.[28] We come into the world with unchosen relationships and obligations, and we continue to exist only in and through them. Human identity is in this respect profoundly illiberal, being rooted in particular kinship structures, existing only in a sequence of generations, always as a child of a family, and invariably as member of particular communities and a stranger to others. At our most basic level, we are therefore beings who are *entrusted.* From the moment we are born and so long as we live, we are heirs to a culture – not as a possibility to be chosen or declined, but as a bequest that allows one to think, imagine, desire, and judge. "Everyone inherits a constituent community," Benoist claims, "which precedes him and which will constitute the root of his values and norms."[29]

Benoist pushes beyond the banal observation that our values and interests reflect our social ecology. His deeper claim, more implied than demonstrated, is that meaning is dependent upon, and in some sense identical with, a cultural inheritance. To be a human being is to be in relationship with people and things that matter to us; and to know who or what I am, I need to understand what has special significance. To this Benoist adds a further suggestion. Since meaning is always socially mediated – it is experienced only through the patterns of a culture – there is no private meaning. All meaning is shared. Benoist means that its experience ineluctably draws on the entire life and experiences of a particular people. How a people lives, thinks, speaks, eats, worships, remembers, imagines, entertains, fights – all this forms the deep and often preconscious background for any personal experience of meaning. Are human beings cognitively captive to their cultures and its patterns of meaning? Benoist argues that cultures embody different answers to ultimate questions, but that they do not form self-sufficient worlds. On the contrary, confrontation with opposing ways of life is an essential component of their own.

If identity depends on belonging, it therefore also depends on exclusion. Benoist's most controversial idea is that social identity is constituted through its ongoing confrontation with what is "Other." It is the most consistent theme across his writing, and the source of his deepest appeal to the radical right. In his early journalism, Benoist often examined work in the biological and psychological sciences that emphasized the place of aggression and hierarchy in animal groups. Over time, as his interests gravitated from the sciences to philosophy, he saw human conflict in a new light.[30] An idea with roots in German philosophy and its peculiar reception in twentieth-century France seems to have provided the key. It held that human beings desire recognition of their equal dignity, and that human identity is profoundly wounded by its absence or distortion. Benoist dropped the concern with liberal equality and applied the idea to entire cultures. He argued that it is collective, not individual, identities that require such recognition.

There is no "we" without a "they," he explained in a 2004 essay. "We are what we are, the way we are, depending on what we are not and the way we are not."[31] Benoist maintained that group confrontation properly takes place through exchange and debate, not conflict. But he exploited a flexible premise in contemporary thought, arguing that human dialogue occurs only on the condition that the "other" truly is and *remains* an "other." For true dialogue to occur, in other words, it must take place where a collective "we" is opposed by a "they" whose differences are recognized as neither superficial nor temporary. Cultures can learn, grow, adapt, and change in light of their confrontation with alien peoples. But this depends, for Benoist, on the continuing and conscious exclusion of rival ways of life. "Exchange presupposes the Other. It only makes sense in so far as it is placed in the presence of the Other."[32]

While Benoist has never made a secret of his admiration for illiberal thinkers, he insists that politics is not founded on the identification of enemies.[33] Hostility is created by the denial of group differences, he argues, not their positive recognition. One of the signature experiences of reading Benoist is witnessing him defend the necessity of confrontation and exclusion for the practice of peace and tolerance. The ambition of this meta-political project is truly astonishing, since it celebrates the values of diversity and difference at the same time that it exalts the importance of hierarchy and exclusion. To hear Benoist, it is almost as if the open society of modernity could be possible only within the closed society of antiquity. This attempted synthesis has led him into psychologically obtuse readings of political history. The atrocities of twentieth-century Europe and its legacy of colonialism—for Benoist they were motivated by an attempt to erase group differences, not to maintain them.[34]

Benoist applies the same logic to contemporary issues. Just as damaging as fear of the "Other" is the desire of liberal societies to integrate them. Whether accomplished through immigration or globalism, this desire reflects a deep discomfort with human heterogeneity and a desire to suppress it. It tolerates other cultures only so long as they come to find a home in the community of liberal societies – only so long as they will inevitably cease to be "other" and be reduced to "sameness." The mistake of liberal multiculturalism is fundamental: to assimilate is to convert, and to convert is to bring about a loss of human diversity. Benoist's most recent political writings tend to mute his paganism, but his rejection of liberal integration remains central to it. He regards the desire to bring outsiders into a shared common life, and to break down long-standing cultural barriers, as a secular expression of Christian universalism. Even in its most profane forms, liberalism therefore continues an evangelical mission to build a global world in which there is no "they" and only a "we," proselytizing not with the message that we are all made in the image of God, but with the dogma that we are all the same.[35]

Benoist's criticism is not that human loyalties are stretched too thin by being attached to cosmopolitan ideals. His objection is moral, not practical: the ideal of a universal community, open in principle to all people, is a moral evil. Because liberal ideals claim to transcend particular times and places, they must bring about a corruption of communal meaning and a perversion of human identities. They tempt a culture into seeing its way of life as universal, while inwardly depleting the particular attachments that make it possible. Benoist is for this reason vehemently anti-American. "The United States is not a country like any other; it is a land without a people," he has written, since it is founded on the illusion of self-evident truths.[36] But whether grounded in biblical religion or its secular surrogates, universal truths cannot animate the spirit of a rooted people and its institutions, art, manners, and values. In Benoist's language, they are abstractions that sever the intimate bonds by which human identity is constituted. They make us strangers even in our earthly homelands.[37]

Anti-Anti-Racism

Nothing has done more to marginalize Benoist in French intellectual life than his positions, stated or suspected, on race. He bears the lasting stigma of early writings, published under a pseudonym, in which he espoused racist views. "The objective study of history," he wrote in 1966, "shows that only the European race has continued to progress since it appeared, contrary to races stagnant in their development."[38] Benoist later repented of his chauvinism, as well as for his support for European colonialism, but he maintained professional connections with racist thinkers well into the next decade. His correspondence includes a revealing exchange, over a five-year period, with a leading American white supremacist and anti-Semite (who shared Benoist's admiration for Yockey).[39]

Although Benoist has publicly disavowed racist ideas for more than three decades, an ambiguity lingers. His writings are often published and translated by small presses with controversial catalogues, and he is known to affiliate with groups with reputations for promoting ethno-nationalism. Across Europe, a network of small magazines and study circles on the far right take inspiration from his writing, and he remains ambiguously active in their work.[40] He is usually careful to note that he dissents from their views on race, as he did in a 2013 address to a white nationalist conference in the United States. But his talk of the importance of "genetic ties" and "carnal homelands" clearly resonates with a new generation of white nationalists, who are eager to claim him as an ally.[41]

Is Benoist a racist? The question is fair, and its answer depends on the definition of the term. If racism means a belief in the inherent supremacy or inferiority of a racial group, Benoist is innocent of the charge, though for idiosyncratic reasons. The problem with racial supremacism is not that it offends racial equality. Benoist, as we will see, rejects egalitarian doctrines too. The problem is that it promotes a form of universalism. To assert that one race is superior in some qualitative respect is to adopt a universal measurement. But because Benoist denies that any such perspective exists – there are no neutral points of view, only the interpretations from within a given culture – he also denies that any racial group can be considered inherently better or worse than another. "The concept of the superiority of one nation, one people, one race, or one civilization is absurd," he cautions.[42]

If racism instead means the belief that race is the primary element in human history, or the determinant of an individual's worth, then Benoist is not a racist either. Though he has shown a curiosity about antiquated forms of racial science, he argues that its views of race are reductive. Race is not a biological "essence" or a theoretical category that can plausibly explain individual or group behavior by itself. To posit a "mechanistic" relationship between race and behavior, he argues, is to make a profound anthropological error.[43] The defining characteristic of human beings is not their genotype or phenotype. It is their culture-making capacity. Benoist is in this sense an idealist, since he believes (and his meta-politics presupposes) that the history of ideas, rather than the history of race or class, is the key to understanding human experience. "The great changes in the history of mankind are above all those that have affected our intellectual life."[44]

But if the racist denies that all races should be regarded as equal, then Benoist is guilty. He professes to be "anti-egalitarian" in both political and racial matters. From his study of ancient democracy he concluded that all political communities are properly founded on inequality (namely that between citizen and noncitizen) and that equality is a mistaken value in any domain. Its error is philosophical: it considers "sameness" more fundamental than difference.[45] Racial equality is therefore a self-undermining value. Its defenders believe they are recognizing and defending the common human worth of different ethnicities. Benoist alleges that the opposite is true. When different racial identities are deemed equal in some essential respect, their diversity is effectively suppressed. They become representatives of a single humankind, expressions of a universal type, rather than being valued in their uniqueness. What equality seeks to protect, it thereby destroys.

Benoist instead proposes a theory of racial identity that he terms "differentialist." Its core principle is that "the irreducible plurality of the human species constitutes a veritable treasure."[46] What he means by the plurality of the human species is not entirely clear, and the ambiguities of the term surely invite radical interpretations. It suggests, at minimum, that perceived differences of race are as much a part of the world's wealth as differences in customs and language. Benoist acknowledges that racial variations are not an unchanging feature of the natural order – there is nothing intrinsically necessary about their present expressions. But for Benoist, their very fluidity is evidence of a fragile value that should be protected as part of the wealth of human "biodiversity." Protected how? Benoist hints that political policies should protect regional identities, but the appeal of differentialism is that it offers a voluntary resolution of racial conflict:

> When the right to difference is clearly presented as a right (of peoples to maintain their identities) and is not seen as an obligation imposed . . . when difference is also presented as what it

> is, and not as an absolute . . . when the principle of difference is vigorously defended to the benefit of all groups, and not only to the advantage of some . . . then one fails to understand how so-called "differentialist" discourse could be considered racist.[47]

In a 2018 article Benoist explained that he is therefore opposed to the ideology of anti-racism. He declared himself "anti-anti-racist" because anti-racist activism only foments what it purports to suppress. It presses communities into thinking that discrepancies in group outcomes are the result of either injustice or backwardness, inviting distrust where a healthier attitude might be an open acceptance of pluralism. Benoist insisted he was not defending the moral or legal legitimacy of prejudice. He boasted that he was only acknowledging, as few are willing to do, the "schizophrenic" effects of an ideology that denies the reality of racial differences while simultaneously promoting heightened racial self-awareness. "We have never spoken so much of races as since we officially eliminated them, resulting in the reinforcement of ethnic categories."[48]

All these issues are showcased in the immigration debates now dominating Western politics. Benoist's position is long-standing, if also equivocal. On the one hand, he defends more restrictive immigration policies and considers immigration an existential threat to European cultures. All nations have the duty to protect their "ethnocultural identity," and that includes recognizing group self-preferences as a natural human good. When asked in 2012 about interracial marriage, for example, Benoist responded that "one cannot be at the same time for race mixing [*métissage*] and for diversity, since the immediate consequence of the first is to reduce the second."[49] On the other hand, Benoist concedes that anti-immigrant xenophobia is destructive of European nations, and that any policy of relocation is impractical. The wisest policy, he advises, is to encourage the cultural separateness of immigrant communities and to oppose their assimilation into European life. The "failed dream" of the American "melting-pot" should serve as a cautionary example of the failures of integration. "I do not believe in assimilation," he concludes. "To assimilate is to lose much in exchange for mostly dreams and illusions."[50]

Identitarian Futures

Identity is a modern problem. A person who inherits a stable moral tradition, who accepts an ascribed social role, and who finds meaning in unchosen obligations – such a person, Benoist claims, cannot experience their identity as a genuine problem. It becomes so only with the uprooting of settled communities and the disappearance of traditional points of reference, which force individuals to look within themselves to discover who they are. For Benoist, this social revolution began with Christianity, matured under liberalism, and culminated in global capitalism. It imagined that individuals find their true identities only by being liberated from familial, civic, and cultural bonds.

Benoist's realization in Paris 1968 was that this millennia-long revolution was about to be challenged by another. Although the New Left soon unraveled, its defense of marginalized groups anticipated new forms of political solidarity. As the group consciousness of women and minorities grew in the ensuing decades, Benoist sought to develop a framework for thinking about the identity of Europeans who, he believed, would inevitably awaken from the spell of liberalism. His writings do not advance an explicit political program, and he disavows all party affiliations, but a movement inspired by his ideas is easy to picture. For it already exists. Identitarianism is a youth movement, existing on the far right of European life, that claims Europe as the rightful and exclusive possession of its historic peoples. Its activists warn that Europeans are being culturally "replaced" by African and Middle Eastern immigrants, who are attempting a reverse colonization of Western nations. Yet identitarianism's ideology repudiates the language of mainstream conservatism, and especially its Christian grammar. It appeals to diversity and differences, not to moral absolutes, and its posture is one of victimhood, not supremacy. Benoist has maintained a critical distance from identitarian activists, but they are unquestionably his ideological children.[51]

Benoist's prediction, now being tested, was that our identitarian age would not feature a conventional contest between "left" and "right." It would stage a confrontation between an "above" inspired by cosmopolitan values and a "below" moved by tribal loyalties. Benoist tells us we will misinterpret the coming clash if we do not recognize its roots in something more primeval than partisan politics. At issue is the spiritual basis of human identities. Should we aspire to build a world on the basis of universal values that remove barriers to greater human inclusion? Or should we defend group identities and resist their assimilation into sameness? Benoist hopes for a peaceful rediscovery of group solidarities, but his proposals for its achievement are riddled with weaknesses. He seems to believe, against the weight of human experience, that social bonds can be strengthened when the values that support them are regarded as culturally relative. He does not seriously consider that his views will result in the continued erosion of traditions, resulting in growing isolation, not deepening fraternity. Nor does he seem aware that in inviting other cultures to adopt his pluralist vision, he is doing what he otherwise forbids – proposing a universal theory of identity whose intellectual home is on the Left Bank.

But whatever their vulnerabilities, Benoist's writings communicate a potent political message, whose hearers need no knowledge of post-structuralism to understand them. Human beings flourish best when they live where their ancestors lived, speak the language their ancestors spoke, and transmit the values and customs their ancestors practiced. European cultures are not unchanging or beyond critique, Benoist argues, but to avoid extinction they must satisfy the human desire for an identity that is collectively entrusted to them, rather than individually chosen by them. Man is an heir by nature, and more than anything he needs to possess shared and stable meanings across time. Benoist is skeptical that his message can find a home in America, a country founded on the political myths that he rejects. But to a Southern writer, also exiled from mainstream intellectual life, Benoist's defense of homelands and peoplehood spoke clearly.[52]

Chapter 5

THE NATIONALIST

"I want to read something to you. I want you to really listen to this." Rush Limbaugh opened his show in a tone normally reserved for a breaking Clinton scandal. But his topic on January 20, 2016 was less sensational, and aimed to provoke reflection rather than outrage. Limbaugh spent the next thirty minutes reading passages from a 5,000-word magazine essay. It warned of "globalist elites" who "manage the delegitimization of our own culture, the dispossession of our people, and disregard or diminish our national interests and national sovereignty." It complained of leaders who "drag the country into conflicts and global commitments" and "preside over the economic pastoralization of the United States." And it encouraged Republicans to campaign on limiting immigration, saving blue-collar jobs, and promising to restore Middle Americans to their central place in the nation's life.

Although the article challenged positions that Limbaugh had spent his career defending, he hailed it as the manifesto for the Trump insurgency that no one, including the candidate, had been able to formulate. It spoke on behalf of Republican voters who found the party's policies irrelevant, its rhetoric dishonest, and its candidates artificial. It described a voting base, misunderstood and exploited for decades, whose lives resembled those of a comfortable "proletariat" more than a propertied middle class. Nationalism and populism, Limbaugh conceded, not free-market orthodoxy, were the heart of the Republican Party and its most viable path to electoral success. The essay was titled "From Household to Nation," and despite anticipating Trump's inauguration exactly one year later, it was not written by an observer of the 2016 primary season. It had been published in 1996 and its author was not available for interview, because he had been dead for over a decade.[1]

At the time of his early death in 2005, Samuel Francis was nobody's idea of the most prescient observer of American politics. He had arrived in Washington twenty-five years earlier with the election of Ronald Reagan, and for the generation of young activists and thinkers who came with him, he was consistently and irritatingly out of step – arguing against free trade during the heyday of globalism, defending entitlements in an era of tax cuts, protesting foreign wars in the face of bipartisan agreement, and questioning Christian influence at the apogee of the religious right. His career had begun promisingly, with early positions at the Heritage Foundation and on Capitol Hill, followed by years as an award-winning columnist at the *Washington Times*. But Francis could not conceal his growing contempt for a movement that, he believed, had failed to understand, let alone challenge, the institutional power of American liberalism.

Francis spent his career as a pathologist of American conservatism, a movement he insisted was terminally ill even during its years of seeming political health. As Republicans won five of seven presidential elections and took control of congress for the first time in forty years, Francis did not see signs of vitality. He saw a movement slowly, and for the most part unconsciously, being assimilated into the structures of power that it professed to reject. His outlook won him admirers on the paleoconservative right, who read his essays in small-circulation journals and applauded his attacks on globalism and defenses of those whom he called, without irony, "real Americans." But his writings won him little access to major conservative outlets, which denounced his views, with varying degrees of accuracy, as racist, chauvinist, and even unpatriotic.[2] Francis spent his last decade as an editor of far-right newsletters, having been fired in 1995 for comments on the morality of slavery. By the end of his life, his remaining defenders included Patrick Buchanan, whose presidential campaigns he advised, and Jared Taylor, a white nationalist who eulogized Francis as the "premier philosopher of white racial consciousness."[3]

Condemned, purged, and marginalized in late life, Francis's reputation has undergone an extraordinary reversal since his death. Journalists on the left and the right, in search of the elusive source code of Trumpism, have looked to his books and essays as its possible origin. They are drawn not only by his prescient politics – a blend of economic populism and cultural nativism – but by his prediction that liberal hegemony would be contested by a "Middle American revolution" led by a nationalist president. Francis's reconsideration will likely not end in redemption – his views on race and religion seem to ensure lasting popular condemnation – but his work, including a massive manuscript discovered only recently, can help us better understand our historical moment and one of its political possibilities. It points to a conservatism whose chief goal is no longer to promote lower taxes at home and liberal democracy abroad. It is to overthrow an existing elite with one drawn from the historic core of the nation. "The real masters of the house," vowed Francis, "are ready to repossess it and drive out the usurpers."[4]

The Science of Power

Samuel Todd Francis shared a family name with Mary Todd Lincoln. He did not advertise the ancestral relation, nor disclose much about his private life. He was born in 1947 in Chattanooga, Tennessee, and raised amid vestigial reminders of an earlier social order. As a child, he visited a grandparents' home that had been built by slaves and still contained places to hide food from Union soldiers. Francis always identified as a Southerner and could write passionately about his heritage, but his views are notable for the absence of regional nostalgia and sentimentality. Francis was a skeptic by temperament and an academic by training. He excelled as a student, studying Latin and Greek in high school before attending Johns Hopkins University and later the University of North Carolina, where he received a doctorate in British history.[5]

If Francis's family background was traditional, his intellectual outlook was strikingly modern, and to a degree that distanced him from his ideological peers. The leading thinkers of postwar conservatism tended to look to ancient and medieval thought for perspectives from which to critique modern society. Francis read deeply in the canon of American conservatism and wrote admiringly about Whittaker Chambers, Richard Weaver, Wilmoore Kendall, and Eric Voegelin, intellectuals who shaped its postwar revival by drawing on classical and religious sources. But Francis had deep misgivings about their philosophical orientation. He acknowledged that American conservatism had developed a sophisticated body of ideas and an articulate body of spokesmen to defend them. But its "proclivity to abstraction" and "philosophical mystifications," he repeatedly charged, had prevented its effective engagement with the bruising realities of political power. "I have less faith in the power of intellectual abstractions than most of my conservative colleagues," he explained.[6]

Francis set off to find a philosophical perspective from which conservative goals could be politically attained and not only theoretically elaborated. He found it in a tradition of political thought that he called "counter-modernism."[7] It included Machiavelli, Montesquieu, and Hume, and placed the study of history over speculative argument. It accepted the materialism and secularism of much modern thinking, and rejected the primacy of metaphysics and theology. But it also countered the political implications that liberals have often drawn from such starting points. It described political life as an unending contest for power, emphasizing the human appetite for it as our overriding social passion. It saw politics not as a sphere where human beings could order their common life through rational deliberation, but as an arena where they invariably seek to dominate each other or to escape domination by others.

Francis was initiated into this school of thought by his study of Vilfredo Pareto, whom he discovered through his developing engagement with the work of James Burnham. Pareto was an early twentieth-century Italian sociologist who sought to construct a "science of power" (in Burnham's words) by studying recurring patterns of change in political history. By observing how human beings act politically, rather than studying how philosophers theorize about it, Pareto believed, it was possible to discern universal laws of social organization. He argued that political societies, save the most simple or primitive, are necessarily dominated by an elite minority. All modern societies function as an oligarchy, and none is genuinely democratic. Pareto was not endorsing an elite in the sense of an aristocracy, and he denied that elites are better, wiser, or more virtuous than other social classes. Elites are simply inevitable, and their composition "circulates" over time according to the changing character of a nation.

Pareto explained minority rule through its use of ideology, whose nature, he argued, is hidden from even its beneficiaries. Elites govern society largely for their own benefit, but they rarely rule through violence or intimidation. They do so through myths, stories, and ideals that justify their domination, endowing it with moral credibility. Pareto was one of the first scholars of ideology, and he carefully examined discrepancies between the abstract content of political rhetoric and its real-world uses. He distinguished between the "formal" and the "real" meaning of political ideology. Its formal meaning is communicated by its explicit concepts and values, and can be understood philosophically. Its real meaning, however, is revealed only through its intended effects on political behavior, which are purposefully disguised by its rhetoric. Although Pareto saw ideologies as self-serving, he did not believe their sole purpose was to deceive the masses. They reflect a genuine human desire, shared by both rulers and ruled, to live together on the perceived basis of morality rather than force.[8]

For Francis, the impotence of American conservatism began to make sense when viewed through the prism of Pareto's work. Why had conservatives, despite election victories, failed to reduce the size of government or stop social liberalization? Francis had a cynical view of Republican politicians, attacking even Reagan at the height of his popularity in office. But he placed the blame squarely on conservative intellectuals, who made two compounding errors. The first was to take the formal meaning of liberalism at face value.

Under the popular slogan "ideas have consequences," they had naively assumed that liberal ideas, rather than the political interests they advanced, were their primary enemy. Francis's writing in the 1980s frequently attacked influential conservatives such as Irving Kristol, George Will, and Richard John Neuhaus, whom he criticized for their "esoteric" preoccupations. While liberal intellectuals were perfecting strategies for seizing institutional power, Francis complained, conservatives were staging conferences to ponder the moral foundations of democracy.[9]

The second error was that conservatives ignored the relationship between their own ideology and its disintegrating social basis. From its birth after the Second World War, the American conservative movement has centered on the defense of individual liberty, free markets, and moral traditionalism. While Francis generally shared these values, he conceded that conservatism, no less than liberalism, was an ideology fused to class interests. Or at least it once was. Although Republicans continued to win elections, it was clear to Francis by the early 1980s that the party was growing detached from its grassroots base. With each election cycle, an ideology rooted in the cultural identity and material interests of the postwar middle class seemed less reflective of voters worried about declining social status and stagnating incomes. Worse, conservatives spoke of America not as a people defined by a shared history and culture, but as an idea defined by universal principles.

Francis's deepening suspicion was that the study of politics is not principally the study of ideas at all. It is the study of power—how it is acquired, lost, used, and concealed by a dominant minority. The primary political question, he concluded, is always which elites shall rule, not whether elites shall rule. The resonance with Marxism was unmistakable, and Francis's writings bore evidence of his having studied not only Marx, but Gramsci and Adorno as well. While he rejected their views on economics and much else, he was impressed by the Marxist understanding of social power and envied the ideological uses to which the American left had put the three political theorists.[10] In time, Francis would outline a radical strategy by which a "new right" might seize back power, but he first asked what transformations in American society had effectively extinguished the "old right." His answer offered a profound revision of the work of the one conservative thinker who, he believed, had nearly seen things right.

Leviathan and Its Enemies

While other conservatives debated the roots of Western culture, Francis studied management theory and the history of corporate governance in the basement of his Maryland home. He showed little interest in political ideas in the abstract, opting instead to study the social and economic structures that he believed supported them. Francis assumed that most Americans held their political views sincerely and were genuinely motivated by them in civic life. Yet he also thought such views were fundamentally shaped by an ongoing civilizational revolution, and that blindness to both its reality and consequences was the crippling failure of the American right.

Francis arrived at this realization through the work of James Burnham, whose 1941 book *The Managerial Revolution* was the seminal influence on his career. Burnham is a central figure in the history of American conservatism, as well as one of the most intriguing. An academic philosopher who became a Communist during the Depression, Burnham's public feud with Trotsky in the 1930s over Stalinism led to his disillusionment with Marxism and transformation into a leading anti-Communist. Burnham eventually left his position at New York University and joined the fledgling *National Review* in 1955, contributing a foreign affairs column until his retirement. In some ways the opposite of Francis, Burnham was a Northerner, a philosopher, and a defender of the Republican establishment. But Francis found in Burnham a key to reading the history of the twentieth century and its sobering implications for American conservatism.[11]

Francis tended to overstate his reliance on Burnham and to downplay their disagreements, but his debt was real. He credited Burnham for discovering, if not quite fully understanding, the great revolution of his time. It was not being waged by statesmen and soldiers on the battlefields of Europe, nor fought by intellectuals in American universities. It was undertaken by administrators and accountants in government and corporate offices. Burnham called it a "managerial" revolution, and his book sold over 200,000 copies. It argued that Marxists were right about the imminent demise of the bourgeoisie, but wrong about the social class rising in its place. Burnham predicted a world of managerial mega-states, ruled by a new elite on the basis of its claims to technological and administrative expertise. Burnham insisted this revolution was inevitable and irreversible, and that conservatives had no choice but to influence its direction from within. Francis accepted Burnham's social vision but rejected its political fatalism, and sought, in effect, to rewrite the book from another perspective.

Leviathan and Its Enemies is the most ambitious book by an American conservative in a quarter century. Found in a stack of floppy disks after Francis died, it was published only in 2016, more than twenty years after it was finished. Francis's personal notes indicate that the book was completed, and he occasionally referenced it in conversation with friends, yet it is easy to see why he made no attempt to publish it in his lifetime. Repetitive and disorganized, its 800 punishing pages display few of his many gifts as a writer. But it is the most substantial thing he ever authored, and essentially synthesized three decades of journalism and private study into a single study. In *Leviathan,* Francis attempted to write the book he believed the conservative movement desperately needed, never possessed, and scarcely knew it lacked. It describes the historical process by which American liberalism captured the institutions of government, education, and media, and how it is invulnerable to conventional conservatism – but exposed to nationalist populism.[12]

Francis wrote *Leviathan* in the early 1990s, when he believed America was entering the terminal stage of a protracted period of social transformation. He called it a "revolution of mass and scale," and compared its importance to the Neolithic transition from subsistence hunting to farming.[13] The revolution was not the product of conscious design. It began with the explosive growth in population at the turn of the previous century, and the subsequent expansion in size of virtually every major institution in the country. *Leviathan* detailed the steady expansion in scale, complexity, and reach of most every sector of American life in the twentieth century. Government, business, education, unions, churches, media, and entertainment were all innovated by a new social pattern. Organizations formerly rooted in local relationships, family ties, and regional cultures became exponentially larger, more impersonal, and more standardized.

The revolution required a new elite to advance it. Its distinctive characteristic, reflective of the institutions it controlled, was its possession of special forms of expertise. The managerial class knew how to run bureaucracies, develop the technologies on which they depended, and communicate their benefits to the masses. *Leviathan* followed Burnham's pioneering work on this new class and described the self-reinforcing process by which growing populations made social reorganization necessary, while new technologies and sciences of management made it possible. But Francis possessed a much sharper eye for political conflict, and he more closely examined the shifting distribution of social power. *Leviathan* chronicled how the managerial revolution explains the major inflection points in postwar American politics. It revealed how the appearance of sharp ideological debates – over the Cold War, civil rights, the New Left, Nixon, the religious right, and globalism – masked conflicts between ascending and declining elites.

Francis's great insight was that disagreements between liberalism and conservatism are best understood as antagonisms between rival elites and their supporters. As in all revolutions, he explained, new elites had to displace those who preceded them, and whose lingering presence hampers the revolution's growth. Francis referred to the older elite as the bourgeoisie, and defined them not by habits or lifestyle, but on the social basis of their power. The bourgeois power base was in private firms and institutions, inherited property, Protestant moral codes, and kinship networks. As a class it dominated American life from the end of the Civil War to the New Deal, but proved incapable, institutionally and morally, of running a diverse mass society. With each generation, Francis observed, its power base shrunk, as its values and institutions were overtaken by a new social model. The bourgeoisie lacked the capacity to stop this trend, Francis argued, but retained the ability to slow it, and its doomed attempt to do so formed the central conflict of American politics.

The purpose of *Leviathan* becomes dramatically clear in its staging of this conflict. Liberalism does what all ideologies do: it rationalizes and justifies the rule of an elite minority. Francis acknowledged that liberalism is a diverse intellectual tradition and that many people believe passionately in its doctrines, even at cost to themselves. But its political function (its real meaning) was to advance the interests of some groups and to suppress the interests of others. Francis examined the policy goals of postwar liberalism in crime, poverty, public health, and education. In every case, he alleged, they aligned with the structural interests of elites. What connected the welfare state, feminism, employment protections, school reform, and liberal internationalism? Francis's undeviating answer was that they serve managerial power through a leveling process of "homogenization." They ensured that consumers had the same tastes, businesses operated in the same markets, students received the same training, and citizens held the same values.

But Francis also alleged more, and here his thinking took a radical turn that would mark his later writings. On its surface, liberalism promoted a fairer social contract and equal protections for all. But beneath its egalitarian aspect, Francis claimed, hid its true vindictive purpose: subverting traditional ways of life. "It is imperative," he wrote, "for elites to challenge, discredit, and erode the moral, intellectual, and institutional fabric of traditional society."[14] Francis wanted his readers to see in liberalism a coordinated project of ongoing cultural dispossession. Its long march through American life, he warned, will eventually target every symbol and institution of an older social order. National loyalty, traditional moral codes, the heroes and founders of American culture—in time, all will be subjected to an accelerating campaign of ideological revision waged through legislation and media. In doing so, Francis explained, liberalism acquires more than moral legitimacy. It draws a replenishing base of support from those it emancipates from outdated social norms.

Conservatives are therefore right to feel forever on the defensive, always resisting the next wave of liberalism, never advancing a positive vision of their own. Yet they are mistaken to believe their ideology can offer serious resistance. Francis's real target in *Leviathan* was not liberalism or the cultural institutions it controlled, and in this lies its sober genius. His target was a conservatism that obtusely thought it could turn the regime to its own purposes. Francis's message, buried under a mountain of policy data, was that American conservatism is the obsolete ideology of a vanquished class, an anachronism whose only licit purpose is to provide a veneer of ideological diversity to American public life. Yet that does not mean the managerial regime is invulnerable to challenge. In the book's closing chapter, Francis hinted that its values are working now to weaken and destroy it from within. And just as the bourgeoisie had given birth to an elite that displaced it, so too are the managers of leviathan midwifing its own enemies, who lack only an ideology and a president to guide them.

Middle American Revolution

How could a political movement rise up to challenge ruling elites? Francis believed it required capturing the anger and resentment of a class of Americans whose interests the managerial revolution had not benefited. He called them "Middle American Radicals" and suggested they would soon form a revolutionary class. He drew from the influential work of sociologist Donald Warren, whose voter surveys in the 1970s had produced a profile of a group of voters, then about a quarter of the electorate, who had not been closely studied. These voters were white and earned incomes in the middle and lower-middle income brackets. They had not attended college and held jobs in skilled and semiskilled professions. Warren found that their political views, while consistent across elections, did not correspond to the platforms of either major party. On the one hand, they defended entitlements and union membership, and were deeply skeptical of large corporations and free trade. On the other hand, they opposed welfare and school busing, and held conservative views on social issues, especially those involving race.[15]

Francis had begun writing on Middle American Radicals (MARs) in the early 1980s and wove them into his maturing interpretation of American politics. He claimed not only that they represented the ignored base of the Republican Party, but that they formed the remaining core of a fractured American nation. According to Francis, MARs had periodically coalesced to become a disruptive force in postwar politics, rising up in support of dissident populists such as Joseph McCarthy, George Wallace, and Richard Nixon. But their electoral influence was sometimes less controversial and more successful. Francis credited Reagan's victories to his ability to cast himself, however misleadingly, as a defender of MAR interests. What were those interests? Francis updated Warren's work by arguing that MARs were neither a distinct economic class nor a political movement committed to abstract principles. He claimed that MARs were united by a common "attitude" or "temperament" about their place in American society.

MARs feel they are members of an exploited class – excluded from real political representation, harmed by conventional tax and trade policies, victimized by crime and social deviance, and denigrated by popular culture and elite institutions. Their sense of grievance points both upward and downward. They believe they are neglected, even preyed upon, by a leadership class who simultaneously favor the rich and the poor over the interests of the middle class. "If there is one single summation of the MAR perspective," Francis wrote, "it is reflected in a statement: The rich give in to the demands of the poor, and the middle income people have to pay the bill."[16] Francis seized on the idea that a major American demographic, so decisive to Republican success, was chiefly motivated not by an ideology, but by a feeling of being disinherited from their own nation. It corroborated his argument that a structural collusion existed between the affluent powerful and the underclass poor, who form a coalition against middle-class values and interests.

While Republicans scrambled for ways to reach minority voters, Francis demanded closer attention to working-class whites instead. He happily granted that they were not typically conservative, at least when measured by the orthodoxies of conservative think tanks and the Republican donor class. It was a feature of MARs, not a flaw, that they could force a reassessment of GOP policies, especially on economic issues, that many voters found repugnant. To his credit, Francis did not idealize their lifestyles or romanticize their struggles. He referred to them as "post-bourgeois" and conceded that if they identified emotionally with traditional American ways of life, they were not a living reservoir of the older bourgeois virtues. Their grasp of American political history, to say nothing of their knowledge of Western culture, reflected the appalling state of general literacy. Francis frequently referred to them as a cultural "proletariat," and noted that many rely on government help in the form of benefits or loans.

As Francis began to imagine a movement built around MAR interests, he cautioned that it might appear ideologically eclectic or even incoherent. MARs tend not to think about politics primarily in terms of the size of government, and they defend neither the minimal state nor the welfare state as a matter of strict principle. What made them "radical," Francis maintained, was their instinctive defense of communal roots and their visceral opposition to cosmopolitan values. MARs are motivated by a particular view of political life, if not a systematic ideology. Francis called it a "domestic ethic," and claimed it as the basis of a viable future conservatism.[17] It reflects a traditional impulse, suppressed by liberal individualism, that sees political life in terms of interlocking loyalties that link the family to the nation. It assesses policies not by an impersonal standard of justice, but by whether they protect and enhance group well-being. Francis believed he had found his vanguard, who lacked only an awareness of its shared interests. It was a social movement, about to be born, that would unapologetically place citizens over foreigners; majorities over minorities; the native-born over recent immigrants; the ordinary over the transgressive; and fidelity to a homeland over cosmopolitan ideals.

After more than a decade of writing about politics, Francis attempted to put his ideas into action. He served as an advisor to Patrick Buchanan's campaigns for the Republican presidential nomination in 1992 and 1996. The two were close friends and had often helped each other on writing projects. Buchanan called Francis "perhaps the brightest and best thinker on the right," and Francis hailed his friend's guerilla candidacy as the start of a "Middle American Revolution."[18] He saw in Buchanan a credible hope for a new ideological synthesis of economic nationalism and cultural populism. His advice, chronicled in his lengthy monthly essays, would be heard on airwaves decades later. He counseled the former

Nixon aide to disavow the label "conservative" entirely and to run as "a patriot, a nationalist, and an America Firster." He encouraged Buchanan to lay at the feet of the bipartisan ruling class a devastating report of national carnage: the breakdown of the family, the coarsening of popular culture, the disappearance of manufacturing jobs, the financialization of the economy, and the lack of a sensible immigration policy. Buchanan gave voice to Francis's ideas in his notorious 1992 "culture wars" speech at the GOP convention in Houston, where he warned the nation was in a war for its very survival.

Although Buchanan won a few million votes, and severely damaged George H. W. Bush's hope for reelection, he never succeeded in attracting broad support. Yet it was not Buchanan's defeat that persuaded Francis of the need for a more aggressive form of racial politics. It was the prospect, in the words of newly elected Bill Clinton, of "a new America of minorities," a nation "without a dominant European culture." Francis contemplated, with mounting terror, what Clinton called "the third great revolution in America," in which whites were projected to become a minority by 2050.[19] Francis's views on race were an open secret and had long stained his professional reputation. It surprised few critics that after years of opposing affirmative action and a holiday for Martin Luther King, Francis finally published, with feigned piety, a biblical defense of slavery, a column that completed his banishment from movement conservatism.[20] Francis spent the last decade of his life in intellectual exile, moving toward an open embrace of racial nationalism. He turned to promoting what he called "white racial consciousness" and opposing the Christian beliefs that he believed prevented its emergence.

Ethnopolitics and the Religious Wrong

Francis saw it as his purpose to awaken a slumbering white majority to a demographic crisis and to warn them what would happen if they failed to respond. As his focus shifted from class to race, his mood turned from confidence to unease. The class he once assumed was instinctively aware of its group interests, and combative in their defense, now appeared oblivious to its looming displacement. "We are witnessing the more or less peaceful transfer of power from one civilization and the race that created and bore that civilization, to a different race," he warned a meeting of activists in 1994.[21] Francis pored over polling data and demographic forecasts, arriving at the conclusion, only later to become conventional wisdom, that the GOP faced possible extinction as a national party. Its attempts to reach minority voters, through a strategy of voter outreach and policy reforms, had been shown to be worse than fruitless; the party had neglected its natural political base in middle-class whites. "Trying to win non-whites, especially by abandoning issues important to white voters," he concluded, "is the road to political suicide."[22]

A more rational strategy, he advised, would enshrine the GOP as the party of white voters, and seek to maximize their turnout through appeals to racial solidarity. Francis sometimes insisted this appeal should be explicit, while other times he cautioned greater tact, but the goal was to trigger in whites a heightened sense of their shared identity and threatened social standing. He identified immigration as the key issue, predicting it would define American politics in decades to come. For Francis, the use of mass immigration by managerial elites was sociologically obvious, though ideologically concealed. It broke down the older cultural and linguistic unity of the nation, creating a deracinated citizenry more easily manipulated by the techniques of liberal governance. Even more important, Francis alleged, by permitting the importation of a new underclass, mass immigration provides the regime with what it needs most—fresh opportunities to engineer solutions to social problems and ethnic conflicts. In doing so, immigration strengthens liberalism's moral legitimacy, which depends on its ongoing ability to dismantle the entrenched privileges of an older America.[23]

Francis denied he was a white nationalist and offered a predictable line of defense. He claimed he was merely following, out of political necessity, a strategy being used by ethnic and sexual minorities. As all politics becomes identity politics, Francis reasoned, whites will have every reason to assert, and minorities will have no grounds to dispute, their common identity and interests as whites. He cautioned that he did not believe race was the primary feature of personal identity, nor did he wish to disenfranchise minorities. But his nods to pluralism sat uneasily with his vision of America as a nation inextricably bound up with white supremacy. Francis was zealous in arguing that the country's past achievements and future existence depended on its ethnic majority. Toward those who believe Americans are united by commitment to a political creed, not by blood and soil, he was indignant. It was a myth, pure "propaganda," that intentionally ignored the nation's roots in the peoples and cultures of Europe. Francis himself did the same to African Americans, preferring to cite, out of sheer provocation, John Jay in *The Federalist* that Americans are "a people descended from the same ancestors, speaking the same language, professing the same religion, attached to the same principles of government, very similar in their manners and customs."[24]

As to why American culture and traditions could not survive

the loss of a white majority, Francis appealed to history and science. There is no evidence in the human past, he asserted, that dominant cultures can continue to flourish in the absence of their dominant racial class. Francis dismissed examples suggesting the contrary, claiming that American culture, at least in its most distinctively Western expressions, cannot be fully transmitted to nonwhites. Francis reached nervously for scientific support, whose fragile intellectual merits he seemed to sense. Race cannot explain the character of American institutions by itself (if race were sufficient to sustain a way of life, he conceded, the crisis would never have arisen). But race is nonetheless essential to its preservation, even though its scientific basis is a matter of dispute. After decades of resisting speculative explanations of human behavior, Francis found himself doing just that, peddling theories of racial biology. "The civilization that we as whites created in Europe and America could not have developed apart from the genetic endowments of the creating people," he claimed, "nor is there any reason to believe that the civilization can be successfully transmitted to a different people."[25]

Francis's interest in racial differences consumed his remaining years, and he turned to examining what he regarded as the unique character traits of whites. He did so out of despair as much as chauvinism, having concluded that political policies, no matter how radical, could not arrest American decline. For Francis, the greatest danger to whites did not come from outside forces or groups. It came from an inner enemy: the mentality of whites themselves. Francis's guiding assumption, across his work, was that races understand their identities in reflexively different ways. He believed, as a seemingly self-evident truth, that non-whites see their identity in primarily racial terms and seek to defend and advance their ethnic group against others. Whites, however, are different. "Whites exist objectively," he claimed, "but do not exist subjectively."[26] Francis took it as an observable fact that whites lack a comparable degree of racial consciousness and racial loyalty. Perhaps most unique, he charged, whites strongly discourage ethnocentrism among themselves, while tolerating, and even encouraging, it among others. "Only whites pretend that pluralism and displacement are good things," Francis complained, "and that the measures necessary to ensure group survival may be immoral."[27]

What are the origins of this mentality? Francis believed the fate of American culture, indeed Western civilization itself, depended on its discovery. He published his own answer in a 1996 article under a pseudonym, and returned often to its themes.[28] It drew selectively from literature, art, and philosophy, attempting to demonstrate that whites place an exceptionally high value on individualism and objectivity, and that such traits combine to account for their past strengths and present vulnerabilities. The argument echoed Spengler. In comparison to other races, Francis claimed, whites encourage vastly greater individual autonomy, a value central to the cultures they have built and largely absent elsewhere. They celebrate those who dare to challenge settled ways, holding up the hero, the rebel, the explorer, the inventor, and the dissident as icons of human excellence. Francis argued that respect for the "Faustian" individual in Western culture has gone hand in hand with a respect for objectivity. From antiquity through the Enlightenment, in its philosophies and sciences, the West has been inspired by a metaphysical vision: that an objective order of reality exists and operates according to universal rational laws. According to Francis, this idea has uniquely encouraged whites to seek ethical ideals universal in their authority and to build political orders impartial in their justice.

Francis later admitted to doubts about the soundness of his claims, but his intellectual scruples were beside the point. His purpose was to confirm a gnawing fear among his racialist readers, and in this he surely succeeded. His message, a potent mixture of flattery and censure, was that the values of Western culture are today being used against it. Its concern for individual dignity and fairness has become "exaggerated" and "distorted" to such an extent that they are now a racial liability. They offer equality to those who wish to rule, tolerance to those who seek to dominate, and refuge to those ready to exploit. Francis argued that this self-destructive mentality is perversely assisted by popular religiosity, which turns cultural displacement into a mark of moral virtue. Although raised in a Protestant family, Francis was not a religious believer and wrote critically of conservatives who thought Christianity could provide philosophical and institutional resistance to liberalism. They fail to see that Christianity has been the most transgressive force in history, and that its values of peace, equality, and justice must inevitably erode every traditional hierarchy. The "religious wrong," as he called conservative Christians, operates under a "false consciousness." Its theology deflects interest away from real cultural problems and allows believers to be morally reconciled to their own dissolution. Modern Christianity is no friend of white Americans, Francis concluded. "Christianity today is the enemy of the West and the race that created it."[29]

Culture War

Francis was the first to admit how unorthodox his conservatism was. It called for deposing elites, not defending existing hierarchies; redistributing social power, not preserving its present division; and undermining ruling norms, not enforcing them. "When I call for the overthrow of the dominant authorities," he explained, "I am not advocating illegal or undemocratic processes, but the war for the culture is nonetheless a radical or even a revolutionary conflict because it involves an almost total redistribution of power in American society."[30] Francis's advice to conservatives was that any hope for victory required first coming to terms with their defeat. He did not mourn that a social revolution had swept away many American folkways. Human history is the story of falling and rising elites. But he was merciless toward conservatives who refused to see reality for what it was. Conservative fantasies about restoring a past way of life are just that. "No one seriously contemplates restoring the republic," he wrote, "because no one has any material interest in it."[31]

But the contest for power is unending, and Francis foresaw the rise of a new political class, born out of the grievances and frustrated pride of Middle America. Francis might have had archaic views on race, but he wrote for the future, hoping to guide the populist coup that would inevitably topple the ossified leadership of the American right. At the time of his passing, he believed this revolt was still "a body without a head," lacking the theorists and politicians who could translate its sense of victimhood into a governing ideology. But the day of its emergence was near and Francis sketched its rough appearance. The new right will have "less use for the rhetorical trope and the extended syllogism than for the mass rally."[32] It will drop the nostalgic language of "Boy Scout jamborees" and speak frankly about rewarding friends and punishing enemies. Francis urged conservatives to build a movement around a president who could channel the passions of forgotten Americans. He again drew from Spengler, encouraging them "to make use of Caesarism and the mass loyalties that a charismatic leader inspires."

—

Francis's writing earned him many critics, few sympathizers, and little influence. His death went largely unnoticed by the media. But as even Rush Limbaugh came to agree, he was indisputably ahead of his time. His hope for a conservatism rooted in economic nationalism and cultural populism is no longer difficult to imagine. It describes the new right-wing parties contending for power across the Western world. In his own nation, Francis anticipated the day when white Americans would confront the swelling demand that their nation, founded on a crime, must atone for its past by opening itself to mass immigration. He believed he had only begun the work of forging the ideological weapons needed in the culture war this portended. Against the "colored world revolution" that both Spengler and Clinton had glimpsed, Francis summoned a revolution of his own, calling on white Americans to set aside their self-harming pieties and begin the cultural reconquest of their own nation. Francis never pretended, not even for a moment, that this was a matter of moral right or justice. It was a matter of power meeting power. "The issue," as he candidly put it, is "who in the wrecked vessel of the American Republic, is to be master?"[33]

Francis prided himself on telling hard truths about political life. But it was he who was deceived. He deluded himself into believing that he was an enemy of leviathan and a friend to his culture, when he was in fact neither. Francis could not see how thoroughly he shared the philosophical assumptions of managerial liberalism. Its denial of transcendence, its rejection of natural law, its anthropological materialism, its skepticism about reason, and its reductive psychology – Francis accepted every one of its doctrines. In his mind, Francis was engaged in a struggle to save civilization and its forgotten wisdom. But in opposing the materialism of the left with a biopolitics of the right, he was trapped in a different intellectual fight – a family dispute over a dwindling and unearned inheritance. Francis was right about many things. He was right that elites seek to subvert institutions and ideas that resist their power. He was right that their promise to deliver us from the unfreedoms of the past will create a tyranny of its own. He was right that that no society is purely liberal, especially the one who aspires to become so.

Yet Francis's best insights were those to which he had no legitimate claim. He stumbled upon them because of the weakness of his ideology, not the strengths of his vision. Francis was blind to the fact that liberalism was most seriously challenged from the religious believers and traditionalists he deplored. Francis accused them of playing by house rules, seeking dialogue rather than conflict, preferring to be "beautiful losers" rather than ugly winners, and his criticism had some merit. But they attempt to do what he could not: to transform the conversation of our common life, opening it to a vision of the world in which truth, virtue, and the highest good have a privileged and not merely permitted place. Francis told us that he sought only to defend Western culture. It is impossible to believe him. His published writings displayed little feeling for literature, art, music, philosophy, or theology. He did not see, because his ideology prevented him from seeing, that our culture's greatest achievements have been made in pursuit of ideas whose power transcends human differences. Francis's failure of gratitude and wonder made him more than incompetent about power. It made him an outsider to his civilization.

Chapter 6

THE CHRISTIAN QUESTION

"As you may know, many young conservatives have left Christianity," the message began. "Although I was raised Catholic, I too am leaving Catholicism, as I believe it is no longer a healthy religion." The young man's name was Dan and he explained why he had apostatized. "The Church has become the number one enemy of Western Civilization. Soon the only people left in Christianity will be third-world immigrants and a handful of self-hating whites." In recent years, I have received many emails like Dan's. The senders' names are possibly phony, but the sentiments they express are unquestionably real. They allege that American churches have betrayed the national interest and weakened the national character. They criticize Catholic bishops for placing the needs of immigrants and refugees over the native-born. They attack Christian intellectuals for fetishizing liberal democracy and human rights. One email even complained about the absence of authentic spirituality in Christian cultures.

The ideological movement these discontents represent is called the alt-right, a name coined less than a decade ago. The nation was introduced to it in August 2016, when Hillary Clinton devoted a campaign speech to deploring its growing influence. "Race-baiting, anti-Muslim, and anti-immigrant ideas are key tenets making up [this] emerging racist ideology," she charged. In any previous election, her speech would have been bizarre. Although the media estimated its followers in the tens of millions, Clinton could not name a single member of a movement that imperiled American democracy. She was not being negligent. The alt-right has no institutions, no money, no political representation, and no traditional media. To what is it committed? The alt-right purports to defend the group interests of white people, who it believes are the compliant victims of a century-long swindle by liberal morality. Its goals are not conventionally conservative. It does not so much question as mock standard conservative positions on free trade, social conservatism, and foreign policy, regarding them as principles that currently abet white dispossession.[1]

Almost everything written about the "alternative right" has been wrong in one respect. The alt-right is not stupid; it is deep. Its ideas are not ridiculous; they are serious. To appreciate this fact, one needs to inquire beyond its presence on social media, where its obnoxious use of insult, obscenity, and racism has earned it a reputation for moral idiocy. The reputation is deserved, but do not be deceived. Behind its online tantrums and personal attacks are arguments of seductive power. The alt-right entices through an appeal for fairness (an ideal it otherwise questions) and a rejection of double standards (a tactic it otherwise condones). It complains that identity politics is a weapon used to protect and celebrate certain groups, and to deconstruct and demean others. It is permissible to speak positively about gay rights, Black Lives Matter, or Zionism, the alt-right claims. But to speak positively about whites as a group, or to express pride in being white, is to invite ostracism and loss of livelihood. Whites should simply enjoy what minority groups possess, the alt-right insists – the ability to organize around a shared identity.

The alt-right's plea for fairness is misleading, however, and masks a different style of political thought. For the movement's leaders are not only openly illiberal and racialist; they are also anti-Christian, flaunting their rejection of Christianity and their desire to convert believers away from it. Greg Johnson, an influential theorist, denies that "Christianity constitutes a viable vehicle for the perpetuation of the European peoples and their culture." Activist Richard Spencer laments that "Christianity provides an identity that is above or before racial and ethnic identity." Academic psychologist Kevin MacDonald argues that contemporary Christianity offers encouragement to an "anti-white revolution." Essayist Gregory Hood claims that "Christianity burns through ties of kinship and blood. It is the essential religious step in paving the way for decadent modernity and its toxic creeds." A major work of alt-right history concludes: "The introduction of Christianity has to count as the single greatest ideological catastrophe to ever strike Europe."[2]

Alt-right thinkers are overwhelmingly atheists, but their worldview is not dismissive of religion or religious questions. On the contrary, to read deeply in its foundational sources is to discover a movement that takes Christian thought and practice seriously. It is the conflicted tribute paid to their chief adversary, whose moral assumptions, they believe, distort our culture and twist our consciences. Against Christianity they make two related charges. Beginning with the boast that Europeans effectively created Christianity – not the other way around – they argue that Christian teachings have become socially and morally poisonous, providing inspiration to ideologies of white disempowerment. They insist that conservatives are therefore tragically mistaken to see in Christianity a buttress against the spread of liberal and progressive values. From the alt-right perspective, such values are the rebellious offspring of Christianity, whose legacy is not the preservation of a cultural past, but the ongoing subversion of traditional ways of life.

Their arguments draw extensively, and sometimes ingeniously, on those we have encountered in this book. They appeal to Spengler's fear that Western culture, having once possessed the strength to shape Christianity in its own image, has slowly succumbed to its egalitarianism. They share Evola's hope of a postliberal order that will restore the archaic basis of social life. They invoke Yockey's belief that critical rationality has been smuggled into the soul of American culture by biblical religion. They echo Benoist's claim that Christian monotheism alienates believers from nature and history. And they rally to Francis's call to build a political movement that dispenses with the false consolations of faith. Their arguments amount to a serious critique of Christianity, a critique whose intellectual merits and political implications deserve close attention. But as we will see, their arguments are far from new and invite Christian theology to reflect on its first confrontation with the political right, as it learns to think about politics in a post-Christian era.

Christian Revolutions

In the nineteenth century, before the phrase acquired a sinister aura, Europeans debated the "Jewish Question." At issue was the place of Jews in a continent being transformed by the ideals of the French Revolution and the pressures of modern nationalism. After centuries of social marginalization, Jews encountered new opportunities, as well as old dangers, in their desire for civic equality. The Jewish Question asked how legal rights could be extended to Jews, as well as how Judaism could actively contribute to modern life and thought. Its most famous response was by Marx, who argued the problem would not be solved by the creation of secular states. Since Judaism was a symptom of human enslavement, and not its material cause, religious freedom for Jews could do nothing to advance human emancipation.

If the Jewish Question concerned the nature of Jewish particularism, the thinkers profiled in this book raise what might be called the "Christian Question." They ask about the nature of Christian universalism and its past and present influence on Western culture. As to that influence, they are overwhelmingly critical, offering arguments that question its contributions to Western values, institutions, and identity. From one perspective, their concerns might appear unexceptional. Criticisms of Christian belief and practice are a central feature of post-Enlightenment thought, and figure so prominently in our intellectual life as to require little elaboration. Christian doctrines are thought by many to be incompatible with the knowledge of the natural sciences, the morality of liberal societies, and the experiences of modern people. A popular assumption is that its teachings inhibit individual freedom, impeding the full use of the mind and the healthy expression of the will.

But in criticizing Christianity, the radical right comes from a radically different perspective, one so opposed to dominant assumptions as to be incompatible with them. To understand these thinkers' angle of vision, and to perceive Christianity as they do, requires more than intellectual curiosity. It requires the ability to see modern society and to read secular arguments from a potentially disorienting vantage point. To state their views succinctly, if also crudely: the radical right critique Christianity for nurturing individual freedom, not suppressing it; for undermining human inequalities, not upholding them; for being rationalistic, not irrational; for its openness, not its exclusivity; for being apolitical, not political; and for living up to its ideals, not betraying them. What is shocking about these formulations is that they invert the conventional terms of intellectual discussion. They accuse Christianity of being the *cause* of modern values it is often blamed for impeding or rejecting.

How did they arrive at such conclusions? Though disagreeing about important issues, their writings display a remarkably consistent interpretation of Christianity, whose general features we are now able to combine into one sketch. They begin by seeing Western societies, even in their most seemingly secular aspects, in robustly Christian terms. Indeed, the world they experience is so haunted by Christian belief, and so thoroughly structured by Christian concepts and assumptions, that it is unintelligible apart from them. Yet their understanding of Christianity is not orthodox. It places far less emphasis on private belief and religious observance than on deeply engrained social practices, the way we experience and belong to social groups. And from this perspective—from that of the deep background assumptions that frame modern life—our secular world is saturated by Christianity.

It is Christian assumptions about human beings, and not Christian beliefs about God, that allegedly make it so. Today, we see human beings as individuals defined by their ability to reason and choose, capacities that endow them with an underlying equality. We see them as persons with interior identities that go deeper than their external relationships. Although these assumptions are largely taken for granted, the radical right argues they are anything but self-evidently true. They are simply tenets of faith, whose forgotten origins lie in Christianity's anthropological revolution. This revolution introduced ideas about human nature and history that gradually transformed Western society, giving rise to the political mentalities that dominate modern life. It saw human beings as individuals, equal in dignity and worth, who are to recognize all men as neighbors. It saw history culminating in a universal community, uniting people from every nation and land.

The radical right argues that this social vision has triumphed so thoroughly that we are scarcely aware of the extent of its victory. Even the most zealous secularist now defends human equality, social justice, and special concern for the marginalized and suffering—ideas that would have seemed foolish, if not incomprehensible, to our pagan ancestors. Christianity is no longer an assumed premise of civic life, and its doctrines are often rejected or derided. But according to the radical right's sweeping claims, its ideological offspring fill our public life. Liberalism is a secular expression of the Christian teaching that the individual is sacred and deserving of protection. Socialism is a secular expression of Christian concern for the poor and downtrodden. Globalism is a secular expression of the Christian hope that history is leading to a kingdom of universal peace and justice. In the past, Christianity spread through religious conversion. In the present, it spreads through secular creeds that preach equality and freedom. It is a sign of Christianity's unique power and enduring hegemony, the radical right claims, that it continues to spread its teachings even while pretending to subvert them.

And here we reach the essence of the Christian Question. Christianity denied what antiquity had serenely assumed: that the strong are destined to rule the weak, that we have no obligations to strangers, and that our identities are constituted by our social status. While this revolution is widely seen as moral progress, the radical right argues that it admits another interpretation, however oblivious we are to it. Nietzsche famously lamented that Christianity made us tender and empathetic, and shifted the burden of proof against the aristocratic sentiment that tolerates cruelties and inequities. In doing so, it burdened us with bad consciences, wounding our self-love and pride. But there is a less elitist and arguably more humane way of mourning the Christian revolution, and the story it tells bids to explain the social distempers of our time. It claims that Christian values, either openly or in secular disguise, uproot human beings from tight social bonds, depriving them of the political, ancestral, and even religious moorings essential for human life. That story goes like this:

Christianity's emphasis on individual faith and conscience places a permanent rift between human identities and political life. Since their true origin and highest loyalty lie with God, Christians are alienated from their earthly communities, whose injustices and exclusions they are compelled to acknowledge. Christianity therefore fractures communal solidarity, dividing society into secular and religious spheres, and identities into the public and private. It attempts to unite humanity through a doctrine of human equality, but this ideal (and its secular substitutes) only worsens social division, rather than healing it. For if human beings share the same nature and purpose, persistent inequalities must be seen as evidence of injustice, not a reflection of natural order. The paradox of Christian individualism, then, is that it undermines the social foundations on which individuals depend.

Christianity also disrupts our relation to history, weakening the traditions and bonds of memory that link us to ancestors. Christian faith is anti-traditional in one glaring respect: it requires gentiles to adopt the sacred history and even the deity of another community, connecting their deepest beliefs to the unique experiences of a foreign people. Perhaps no aspect of Christian life is so spiritually deracinating, so subtly subversive of human customs. In requiring this of gentiles, Christianity revolutionized their experience of time, turning history into a story defined by its overcoming. Believers live in anticipation of a heavenly kingdom that will redeem their fallen past, not in the veneration of an earthly golden age that will be restored. As a result, Christian ideas have created a world where politics increasingly moves in one direction: by repenting of the past and its accumulated transgressions. For what is modern politics, in virtually all its forms, but the reenacting of this original Christian drama? The tragedy of Christian history, then, is that leaves us trapped in the present, having severed our roots in the deep past.

If Christianity ruptures social unity and memory, it also undermines religiosity. No idea so secularizes the world, and so robs it of enchantment, as the Christian doctrine of creation. The earth was once full of gods, but Christianity banished them, setting society on a path that led inevitably to secularism. In claiming that the ultimate source of truth and value exists in a transcendent realm, it effectively made the world profane. It emboldened human beings to investigate nature and to dispel its mysteries without fear of divine punishment. Disenchantment gave human beings extraordinary power over nature, but it came at a steep cost. In slowly ridding the world of mystery and myth, Christianity tore the sacred canopy from communal life, crippling our ability to experience the divine in nature. The irony of Christian faith, then, is that it not only abolished rival spiritual practices; it drained the cosmos of religious meaning.[3]

Is this story about Christianity at all persuasive? At first glance, its sweeping claims are not. The narrative it tells is both simplistic and overdetermined. It interprets the past in terms of the present, attributing to Christianity a modern mindset that is liberal, secular, and nonconformist. In doing so, it ignores the diversity of Christian practice and its defenses of social hierarchies. It also overlooks liberal ideals that have emerged apart from Christian inspiration, and the contributions of non-Christian religions to Western society. But however dubious its particular claims, this story succeeds in raising an important theological question, whose salience will grow in a secular age. It concerns Christianity's peculiar form of universalism and its revolutionary consequences. For it is Christianity's conception of *transcendence,* the radical right argues, that is the hidden origin of our most serious cultural pathologies.

Christianity gave birth to a culture that grounds its legitimacy outside of itself, and in doing so slowly lost its own identity. In a former age, our civilization was built on the belief in God as the transcendent source of truth and goodness. In a secular age, we tend to locate transcendence elsewhere. We venerate ideals of justice, equality, and freedom with a respect formerly accorded to God. But in either age, this story alleges, we strive to order our common life toward values whose origin and validity do not depend upon who we are – that are not fundamentally an expression of *us.* For some, this has inspired the best of Western culture. It has nurtured its openness, diversity, and capacity for self-criticism and change. But for those who raise the Christian Question, it is the original wound of our civilization. It denies us an innate identity and a unique destiny, requiring us to live a life that is not really our own. It disorients our natural instincts and disrupts our natural attachments, leaving us increasingly incapable of defending them. Such is the legacy of the Christian revolution.[4]

A Post-Christian Right

Today it might seem unlikely that a mass political movement could take inspiration from anti-Christian arguments. It is difficult to imagine a generation of students undergoing conversions while reading Julius Evola or Francis Yockey, as they once did with Marx or Marcuse. It is even harder to imagine the Christian Question defining public debate as the Jewish Question once did. What seems more likely, indeed what seems probable, is that these authors will prove to be guides to understanding political attitudes and passions that already exist. An anti-Christian right is difficult to conceive, but a post-Christian right is struggling to be born. Its arrival is far from inevitable. But should it come to maturity, its appearance ought not to surprise us. Its voters will not be waving copies of Spengler, Evola, Yockey, Benoist, or Francis. But they will be giving voice to their ideas all the same, expressing through protest and anger the thoughts of philosophers they have never heard of, and whose arguments we have long presumed to ignore.

A post-Christian right will speak a distinct ideological language. It will display little theoretical elegance, and its rough inflections will reject the polished tones of traditional conservatism. It will not speak reverently of free markets, individualism, or constitutionalism. It will not genuflect to the natural law or the moral pieties of the "Judeo-Christian" tradition. For what is prosperity without a patrimony, and freedom without a home? It will instead give defiant expression to primordial passions, once disciplined by religion, that liberalism tried to repress – about preserving cultural differences, punishing enemies, and deposing disloyal elites. It will lack a way of describing the solidarity that it seeks, and it will thrive on naming the dangers it claims to expose. But should a post-

Christian right seek unity in what binds human beings from below, rather than what unites them from above, a decisive step will have been taken. It will represent an attempt to undo the Christian revolution by severing the connection between Western culture and transcendence.

A post-Christian right could take two very different shapes, exploiting different openings in a crumbling liberal consensus. It could appear in a semi-pagan form, whose general outlines are glimpsed in authors in this book. It would claim to have recovered cultural traditions and national symbols, boasting to have restored a patrimony to those it had been wrongly denied. It would be unlike reactionary movements of the past in one essential respect, however. Its ideology would echo the progressive left, borrowing not only a conceptual vocabulary but, much more important, a degree of moral legitimacy. Its appeals to diversity, difference, and victimhood would therefore blunt charges that it espoused supremacist ideas. Indeed, it would almost certainly denounce these ideas vehemently, insisting that it had been dispossessed by the supremacism of liberal ideologies. In some countries, a post-Christian right might even ally with an ecological left, creating a brown-green coalition that aimed to protect what the alt-right calls "human biodiversity."

But a post-Christian right could also appear in a more deceptive form, exploiting openings on the religious right rather than the secular left. It could clothe itself in Christianity, claiming a religious mantle for its defense of ethnic or cultural identity. Not all nationalisms are anti-Christian, of course, but some are. The theological marks of a false nationalism include: the idea that an individual is Christian in virtue of being born into a particular ethnicity or nation; the idea that a people is innately Christian in virtue of its history or culture; the idea that Christianity is an inheritance a people possesses as its own, rather than a gift they share with others; the idea that a Christian community is closed to those outside its ethno-cultural boundaries. All these ideas understand Christianity as something that originates from *within* a people, as an expression of their identity, rather than something that comes to it from without. Spengler regarded Christianity as the finest creation of the European soul, and it is the perennial temptation of religious nationalists to imagine the same.[5]

Although some of these scenarios might seem distant, Christian theology must be prepared to confront a post-Christian right with the same vigor that it has challenged the secular left. Yet it must do more than identify the movement's intellectual errors and guide the political judgments that resist their influence. It must also offer an account of human identities that takes the alt-right's criticisms seriously. To argue that a post-Christian right is illiberal, bigoted, or simply immoral might well be correct, and Christians must play an essential role in combating racism. But it is also insufficient. Its thinkers simply do not share the assumptions that give these terms popular credibility, and their refusal to accept them is a matter of philosophical principle rather than verbal evasion. The alt-right seeks a thicker account of what we are meant to be and serve as a people, and it is not alone in invoking ethnic solidarities as a cure for our fraying civic bonds. It distorts many truths, through both malice and ignorance, and leads young men into espousing views and defending authors they scarcely understand. Yet Christians can learn from their distortions, and in doing so show how Christian theology, whose failings have contributed to the movement's rise, might also be its remedy.

The Christian Race

Christianity turns subjects against rulers, the weak against the strong, and the living against the dead – Christians can recognize these as the oldest accusations made against their faith. As Christianity spread through the Roman Empire in late antiquity, it encountered resistance by pagans who saw its teachings as a cause of social decline. And if we listen to the last generations of pagans, worried about the tending of the ancestral flame and the deities of hearth and home, we hear familiar laments. We hear them worry about the severing of ancestral bonds, the neglect of family customs, and the crumbling of social hierarchies. We hear them mourn the novelty of Christianity, its elevation of the individual, and its suspicion toward civic traditions. Their fear is a primal one – that of ancestral annihilation.[6]

Early Christian writers took these arguments with a seriousness that suggests many believers shared these fears, which anticipate so many postliberal anxieties. They acknowledged that their young faith was open to all people and that, unlike many closed religions, admittance to its rites required no particular social or civic background. "Christians are indistinguishable from other men either by nationality, language or customs," a second-century CE writer observed. To them, "every foreign country is their homeland, and every homeland is foreign."[7] Early Christian thinkers drew inspiration from the New Testament's vision of a world in which differences of race, class, and sex would be healed. "There is neither Jew nor Greek, neither slave nor free, male and female: for you are all one in Christ Jesus," Saint Paul instructed the church in Galatia. This early Christian universalism also insisted on the primordial unity of the human family, arguing that "God has made of one blood all the nations of the world."[8]

But did Christian faith transcend every ethnic or racial category? According to some Christians, the answer was more complicated than one might assume, and their ideas open up a fascinating path for Christian thought in its confrontation with a post-Christian right. In response to fears of ancestral loss or betrayal, early Christian thinkers promised believers an astonishing consolation. Their true ancestors would not be lost, nor their traditions forgotten. They would be restored. Conversion to Christianity brought about a transformation in ethnic identity, making believers members of a family that stretched back to the dawn of human history. This ancestry included not only Christians, both saintly and ordinary, who persevered in faith. It also included faithful Jews and virtuous pagans who had lived upright lives without knowing the full truth about God, through no fault of their own. For these thinkers, Christianity was not simply a religion of individual faith. Christianity was a *race.*[9]

What did it mean to be a Christian in a world of Romans, Greeks, Egyptians, and Jews? In defining themselves in relation to other peoples, early Christian thinkers made use of culturally available concepts. For Clement of Alexandria, Justin Martyr, Origen, and others, it included the idea that Christians formed a *genos* or *ethnos,* terms that we now translate as "race," "people," or "nation." In antiquity, these terms lacked fixed meanings, but they generally classified groups by their biological kinship, as well as their common language, customs, and territory. What is fascinating, and at first glance strange, is that major Christian thinkers also applied them to Christians, who seemed to share none of these characteristics universally. Appearances to the contrary, Christians were a people of shared backgrounds and kinship, making them a *genos* or *ethnos* in their own right. These thinkers boasted that Christians even possessed the most ancient and most distinguished pedigree of all peoples, a claim that can only have amused the ancient peoples of the world. What is more, this pedigree included not only Jesus and the patriarchs of Jewish scripture, but the wisest philosophers of antiquity, who sought the truth about God with a sincere heart. All were part of the "race of the saved," as one scholar has put it, because they had rendered sincere worship to God.[10]

We are likely to find this confusing, if not absurd, and too dismissive of other forms of religious universalism. Even if race is in some important sense socially constructed – in the sense that its boundaries and meanings reflect human judgments – we are inclined to reserve the term for those sharing a degree of biological kinship. Yet Christian thinkers were aware of the extraordinary nature of their genealogical claims, and they invoked scripture to defend them. They drew on Paul's idea, understandably shocking to Jews, that Christians acquire Abraham as an ancestor, becoming descendants of Israel through faith.[11] They imagined that Christians were reborn by being grafted onto a new family tree, exchanging the traditions of their earthly fathers for those of their forefathers in faith. But was it only a spiritual lineage that early Christians imagined they shared with faithful Jews and noble pagans? Astonishingly, no. For some theologians, since the humanity of all believers, indeed all the saved, was included in the flesh of Jesus, Christians had a kind of sacramental kinship with all those united in his mystical body.

There are few reasons to think this understanding of race could be revived today, and many reasons to believe it should not be. Non-Christians will find it unintelligible and Jews will find it troubling. These arguments are nonetheless worth revisiting, and not only because they were made in an age with parallels to our own – a time of mounting worry over blurring borders, changing demographics, and deteriorating empire. They should interest Christians because of what they reveal about the breadth of the early Christian imagination. Christian theologians in the first three centuries of the Common Era wanted to show that Christian faith was concerned not only with individual salvation in the future and personal holiness in the present. It also healed one's past. The Christian revolution did not make believers into orphans, cut off from an ancestry and estranged from a culture. Christians were members of a people whose roots were as deep as human history, and whose genealogy boasted of saints, sages, and heroes with whom they were related through God.

Christians need not call this community a "race" to make stronger claims about the way it binds them together across time. Christians believe, after all, that this identity expresses them at the deepest possible level, corresponding to their true selves in a way that their ethnic, national, and even familial identities cannot. If human beings are what Christians claim them to be – embodied souls, united through an incarnate God – then this people restores their true *ethnos,* since they receive from it life in the spirit. Christianity in the third millennium is a global religion whose greatest vitality is among those Spengler called the "colored world." For just this reason, Christians ought to be mindful of a social vision glimpsed in its first centuries. It urges Christians to be skeptical about the existence of biological race, though not because they have been persuaded by natural science or postmodern philosophy, and not only because they are heedful of the ways it has inspired human cruelty. It prompts Christians to skepticism because its vision affirms the higher truth, shared by other religious traditions, that humans are made for divinity, and that nothing merely material is fully human. Christians need not amend their family trees to include Christ, Abraham, and Socrates, and they need not deny that non-Christian religions have glimpsed the same truth. But in an age of racial anxieties they might be more willing to bear witness to an ideal of ethnic solidarity that is open to transcendence, rather than closed to it.

Memory and Identity

Like believers in late antiquity, Christians need to be willing to see their cultures, including their proudest achievements, through the eyes of their most unforgiving critics. Doing so requires that they resist the temptation, however powerful, to dismiss their critics' ideas as motivated solely by prejudice or hatred. The radical right can be ignored or marginalized for a time, and we can hope that its season will not soon arrive. But it represents a perennial possibility in our political life, and where social changes continue to open new intellectual spaces, its opportunities for expression will undoubtedly grow. Its ideas do not cease to animate human minds when they cannot be openly expressed and debated, and it is no credit to us if we succeed in repressing them without first understanding them. We cannot know what we affirm without knowing what we deny, and we cannot know who we are if we do not know what other ways of life are possible.

Young men like Dan are right to feel an erosion of belonging, and they are right to look with disdain at intellectual traditions that fail to take their longings seriously. That their need for experiences of shared identity and common purpose has gone unmet should concern us all, and not just its frightening expression. It is a fantasy to believe those needs can be met through imagined affinities of blood. But it is no less a fantasy to believe they will be met through a deeper embrace of the values and practices of the open society. For there are human needs that liberalism cannot possibly satisfy—needs that it now struggles even to acknowledge. Our need to bond with a family, community, and nation to the exclusion of others; our need to protect and pass on an inheritance; our need to celebrate exceptional human beings and inequalities of achievement; our need to experience self-transcendence through self-sacrifice; our need to exhibit loyalty to those specially like us—these are needs of the human spirit that liberalism has often chosen to ignore or impugn.[12]

Liberalism aspired to order society around a vision of human beings, abstracted from all attachments, whose fundamental needs are for prosperity, peace, and pleasure. It imagined human beings as rights-bearing individuals who could pursue their own understanding of the good life. If liberalism is in crisis, it is because this picture of human life has proven to be impoverished. Human beings are not defined through acts of individual choice and self-expression alone; they are social creatures who find meaning through relationships they have not chosen and responsibilities they cannot relinquish. Human identity is in this respect irreducibly illiberal, being embedded in lines of kinship and descent, existing only in a sequence of generations, always as a child, and invariably an inheritor of a particular cultural and social patrimony. It is an irreducible part of our nature, an absolute given, that we owe our existence to parents and peoples we did not originally choose.

We can no longer believe that human identity is determined by matters over which we have no say. But we also find it impossible to credit the myth that our identities can be sustained by free choice and enlightened self-interest alone. It has become clear that expanding our freedom of choice has left many people alone and unhappy, nostalgic for the structured communities and thick identities that former generations possessed. Liberalism was right to affirm that we are capable of self-governance, an ideal it inherited from classical and Christian thought. But it was wrong to see our rootedness in particular communities and traditions as obstacles to human freedom, rather than as natural conditions for its attainment. For it is the essence of our creaturely condition, as well as human happiness, that we learn to order these bonds to real human goods, turning the passions that weave the fabric of life into the virtues that clothe it with dignity. Our loyalties to a nation, culture, or people can, of course, become dangerous when severed from truths that transcend them. But they are not parochial loyalties that need to be exchanged for more cosmopolitan ones. They are essential aspects of every human life, and to ask people to apologize for what they are right to value, and to be ashamed for what they are right to need, is to tempt political catastrophe.

Our politics will inevitably seek out new forms of solidarity, looking for ways to bind together what we once thought wise to emancipate. It will be inspired by the recognition that individuals cannot fill the content of life by themselves. It will be a time of renewal only if we have found the language to guide the positive, and not only the destructive, meaning of aspirations that have been frustrated. At its best, Western culture, like all the world's great cultures, is animated by this aspiration. In this, it bears the living legacy of Christianity, which bequeathed to it a tension between particular and universal loves. Christianity acknowledges our natural preferences for the familiar and the known. It teaches that, as finite creatures, occupying particular points in time and space, our earthly attachments must always be partial in their embrace. But Christianity also teaches that we must learn to love what is good, a capacity requiring us to order our earthly loyalties to what is infinitely beyond them. Our politics has often attempted to collapse this tension, but Christianity insists on maintaining it. In an age of tribalism, it witnesses to our common nature. In an age of globalism, it reminds us of the dignity of our finitude. These are truths that Christianity does not alone know. But they are truths that, for many in our culture, it still knows well.

In his final book, *Memory and Identity,* John Paul II reflected on the Christian meaning of our earthly homelands. He was responding to the experiences of a particular people, in this case Poles, and their recent suffering under ideologies of the radical left and right. He sensed their growing fear that what totalitarianism had failed to achieve thorough violence – the erasure of their cultural identity – liberalism might accomplish through their consent. The pope noted that Poles, like all peoples, needed an understanding of their identity that rooted them in their past without closing them to the future, and that opened them to encounter with others without forfeiting what made them unique. He denied that Christians have no "native land" in this life, and he defended the nation as a natural community. Against those seeking a more homogenous world, he urged Poles to preserve their language, memories, and religious traditions. Only a culture that respects itself can show respect to others, and only a culture that preserves itself has something to share. The "spiritual self-defense" of one's culture, he argued, is part of our moral obligation, commanded by God, to honor our fathers and mothers.[13]

But any people, he concluded, will become an idol if its cultural inheritance is not oriented toward, and inwardly transformed by, a divine inheritance. "The inheritance we receive from Christ," the pope wrote, "orients the patrimony of human native lands and cultures toward an eternal homeland." Christianity midwifed many nations and can renew their cultures still, but that is the subject of another book. For now it must suffice to conclude: the alt-right, and the traditions on which it draws, cannot. Its understanding of identity is reductive, and its rejection of religious solidarity is premature. It speaks of tradition, while transmitting no traditions. It guards a false patrimony, while destroying real ones. It seeks divinity, while desecrating its sacred signs. Its mistake is fundamental and tragic. Race offers no inheritance, and its mere preservation reflects no human achievement. Our stories, art, music, institutions, and religious traditions – unlike race, they are transmitted only through special efforts of human intelligence and love. They are a bequest of spirit, not of blood.

The thinkers of the radical right speak an alluring language. Where liberalism offers security and comfort, they promise adventure and conflict. Although the struggle they envision is so far imaginary, it does not matter: they have a sounder view of human needs and deeper awareness of human possibilities. No serious account of political life can be built solely on our needs for life, liberty, and property. For we desire more than small pleasures in the routines of life. We also seek great challenges in the face of death. And here Christianity speaks another and no less demanding language. "When Christ calls a man," wrote another twentieth-century dissident, "he bids him come and die," and in dying, to receive true life. For Christians, the problem with Faustian men is not the vaunting heroism of their aims. It is the pitiable smallness of their goals. We are not meant to merely aspire to the infinite. We are called to participate in it – to be, in a word, deified.

NOTES

INTRODUCTION

1. For Viktor Orban's July 2014 speech on building an "illiberal state," see Czaba Toth, "Full text of Viktor Orbán's speech at Băile Tuşnad (Tusnádfürdő) of 26 July 2014," *Budapest Beacon,* July 29, 2014, accessed July 26, 2018, https://budapestbeacon.com/full-text-of-viktor-orbans-speech-at-baile-tusnad-tusnadfurdo-of-26-july-2014.

2. For exceptions, see Zack Beauchamp, "The Anti-liberal Moment," *Vox,* September 9, 2019, https://www.vox.com/policy-and-politics/2019/9/9/20750160/liberalism-trump-putin-socialism-reactionary; Park MacDougald, "The Catholic Debate over Liberalism," *City Journal,* Winter 2020; and Daniel Luban, "Among the Post-liberals," *Dissent,* Winter 2020.

3. See George Hawley, *Making Sense of the Alt-Right* (New York: Columbia University Press, 2017).

4. For histories of the movement, as well as discussions of ongoing controversies over its members and shared beliefs, see Walter Struve, *Elites Against Democracy: Leadership Ideals in Bourgeois Political Thought in Germany, 1890–1933* (Princeton, NJ: Princeton University Press, 1973); Jeffrey Herf, *Reactionary Modernism: Technology, Politics and Culture in Weimar and the Third Reich* (New York: Cambridge University Press, 1984); Erich Heller, *The Disinherited Mind: Essays in Modern German Literature and Thought* (Orlando, FL: Harcourt Brace, 1975); and Kurt Sontheimer, "Anti-democratic Thought in the Weimar Republic," *The Road to Dictatorship: Germany, 1918–1933,* ed. Theodor Eschenburg, trans. Lawrence Wilson (London: Oswald Wolff, 1964). On the movement's critical views of Christianity, see the influential study of Armin Mohler, *Die konservative Revolution in Deutschland 1918–1932: Grundriss ihrer Weltanschauungen* (Stuttgart: Friedrich Vorwerk Verlag, 1950), pp. 117–120.

5. James Angelos, "The Prophet of Germany's New Right," *New York Times Magazine*, October 10, 2017.

6. I borrow the term from Eric Kaufmann, *Whiteshift: Populism, Immigration, and the Future of White Majorities* (New York: Abrams Press, 2019).

7. As noted by Mark Lilla, *The Shipwrecked Mind: On Political Reaction* (New York: New York Review Books, 2016), pp. x, xv.

8. Leo Strauss, "German Nihilism," ed. David Janssens and Daniel Tanguay, *Interpretation* 29, no. 3 (1999): pg. 358. See also Leo Strauss, *On Tyranny* (Ithaca, NY: Cornell University Press, 1963), pg. 224.

CHAPTER 1. THE PROPHET

1. After meeting Hitler on July 25 in Bayreuth, Spengler was reported to have remarked, "When one sits across from him, one does not have even one single time the feeling that he is significant." John Farrenkopf, *Prophet of Decline: Spengler on World History and Politics* (Baton Rouge: Louisiana State University Press, 2001), pg. 237.

2. Oswald Spengler, *The Hour of Decision,* Part One: *Germany and World-Historical Evolution,* trans. Charles Francis Atkinson (New York: Alfred A. Knopf, 1934), pp. 95, 176, xiv. The book was originally published as *Jahre der Entscheidung. Deutschland und die weltgeschichtliche Entwicklung* (Munich: C. H. Beck, 1933).

3. Spengler, *Hour of Decision,* pg. 145.

4. Spengler, *Hour of Decision,* pg. 210.

5. Spengler, *Hour of Decision,* pp. 169, 205.

6. See Anton Mirko Koktanek, *Oswald Spengler in seiner Zeit* (Munich: C. H. Beck, 1966); Gilbert Merlio, *Oswald Spengler: Témoin de son temps* (Stuttgart: Akademischer Verlag Hans-Dieter Heinz, 1982); Sebastian Maass, *Oswald Spengler: ein politische Biographie* (Berlin: Duncker & Humblot, 2013).

7. Oswald Spengler, "Pessimismus?," in *Reden und Aufsätze* (Munich: C. H. Beck, 1938), pg. 75. In the same essay Spengler expressed regret over the title of his book, remarking that it should have been titled *The Fulfillment of the West.*

8. Thomas Mann, "Über die Lehre Spenglers," in *Bemühungen. Neue Folge der gesammelten Abhandlungen und kleinen Aufsätze* (Berlin: S. Fischer, 1925). Martin Heidegger, *Off the Beaten Path,* trans. Julian Young (New York: Cambridge University Press, 2002), pg. 246. Northrop Frye, "The Decline of the West," *Daedalus* 103, no. 1 (1974): pp. 1–13. Egon Friedell's history of modern Europe paid particularly high tribute: "One has to climb very high in the world's literature to find works of such scintillating and exuberant intellect, such triumphant psychological vision, and such a personal and suggestive, rhythmic cadence as his *Decline of the West*." Egon Friedell, *A Cultural History of the Modern Age: Renaissance and Reformation* (New York: Routledge, 2017), pg. 37.

9. To be more accurate and chronological: Pharaonic Egypt, ancient Mesopotamia, pre-imperial China, Vedic India, classical antiquity, "Arabian" culture, pre-Columbian America, and Europe.

10. Oswald Spengler, *The Decline of the West*, vol. 1, *Form and Actuality*, trans. Charles Francis Atkinson (New York: Alfred A. Knopf, 1926), pg. xiv. Published originally in Vienna and then in Germany as *Der Untergang des Abendlandes: Gestalt und Wirklichkeit* (Leipzig: Braumüller, 1918), it was republished in a revised edition in 1922, shortly after the release of its second volume, *Der Untergang des Abendlandes: Welthistorische Perspectiven* (Munich: C. H. Beck, 1922).

11. Human history has "no aim, no idea, no plan." Spengler, *Decline of the West*, 1:ii.

12. See August Messer, *Oswald Spengler als Philosoph* (Stuttgart: Strecker und Schröder, 1924), pp. 53 ff. See also Farrenkopf, *Prophet of Decline*, pg. 97.

13. Spengler, *The Decline of the West*, 1:107. Spengler maintained that cultures develop only in a certain natural ecology and that their unique life-forms are rooted, like plants, in a particular soil, landscape, and climate. He did not reveal how they come into existence to begin with.

14. "Life has an aim. It is the fulfillment of that which was ordained at its conception. But the individual belongs by birth either to a particular culture or only to the human type [biological species] in general – there is no third unit of being for him." Oswald Spengler, *The Decline of the West*, vol. 2, *Perspectives of World History*, trans. Charles Francis Atkinson (New York: Alfred A. Knopf, 1928), pg. 48.

15. Spengler, *Decline of the West*, 1:131.

16. Spengler was widely criticized for his view that cultures are closed worlds. Isaiah Berlin thought Spengler had misused the work of Vico and Herder, and he dismissed Spengler's view of cultures as "impenetrable bubbles." Isaiah Berlin, *The Crooked Timber of Humanity: Chapters in the History of Ideas*, 2nd ed., ed. Henry Hardy (Princeton, NJ: Princeton University Press, 2013), pg. 11.

17. "Mankind? It is an abstraction. There are, always have been, and always will be men, and only men." Spengler, *Decline of the West*, 1:44. Spengler was paraphrasing Goethe.

18. Spengler, *Decline of the West*, 1:47. No chapter of *Decline* is as challenging as its attempt to explain diverse forms of mathematics.

19. Spengler, *Decline of the West*, 1:345.

20. Spengler, *Decline of the West*, 1:15.

21. "Faustian man differs from all others in his insatiable will to reach the infinite. He seeks to overcome with his telescope the dimensions of the universe, and the dimensions of the earth with his wires and iron tracks. With his machines he sets out to conquer nature. He uses historical thinking to take hold of the past and integrate it into his own existence under the name of 'world history.' With his long-range weapons he seeks to subdue the entire planet, including the remains of all older cultures, forcing them to conform to his own pattern of life." Oswald Spengler, "Prussianism and Socialism," in *Selected Essays,* trans. Donald White (Chicago: Regnery Press, 1967), n.p.

22. Spengler, *Decline of the West,* 1:309, 341.

23. Spengler, *Decline of the West,* 1:183.

24. Spengler, *Decline of the West,* 1:319.

25. Spengler, *Decline of the West,* 2:298.

26. Spengler, *Decline of the West,* 1:40.

27. Weber did see an important place for "charismatic" individuals in the development of bureaucratic rationality and modern social processes. See Max Weber, *Essays in Sociology,* trans. C. Wright Mills and H. H. Gerth (New York: Oxford University Press, 1958), pp. 51–55.

28. In a letter from early 1919, Spengler praised Hegel as a defining expression of the "Western Mind." Oswald Spengler, *Spengler Letters: 1913–1936,* trans. Arthur Phelps (London: George Allen & Unwin, 1966), pg. 72.

29. "The hero is indifferent to death and the saint indifferent to life." Oswald Spengler, *Aphorisms,* trans. Gisela Koch-Weser O'Brien (Regnery: Chicago, 1967), pg. 30. For a Hegelian reading of Spengler, see Ricardo Duchesne, *Faustian Man and Multicultural Society* (London: Arktos, 2017), pp. 155–165. For an influential reading of the aristocratic dimension of Hegel's parable, see Alexandre Kojève, *Introduction to the Reading of Hegel: Lectures on the* Phenomenology of Spirit, comp. Raymond Quenau, ed. Allan Bloom, trans. James H. Nichols (Ithaca, NY: Cornell University Press, 1969), pp. 45–46.

30. Oswald Spengler, *The Decline of the West,* Volume One, pg. 358.

31. The criticism, leveled by some critics, that Spengler's imagination was restricted to Germany is patently absurd. His travels in Italy and France, as well as his command of languages, allowed him to display a deep and broad knowledge of European art and literature. For one such criticism, see Hans Weigert, "Oswald Spengler, Twenty-Five Years Later," *Foreign Affairs* 21, no. 1 (1942): pp. 120–131.

32. "These meditative discoverers in their cells, who with prayers and fastings wrung God's secret out of him, felt that they were serving God thereby. Here is the Faust-figure, the grand symbol of a true discovering Culture." Spengler, *Decline of the West,* 2:501.

33. This is not the world of the pagan antiquity or the Bible. Of this aspiration, Spengler alleges, "neither Homer nor the Gospels know anything whatever." Spengler, *Decline of the West,* 1:186.

34. Spengler, *Decline of the West* 1:344.

35. Spengler credits Nietzsche for giving him the "questioning faculty" and at one time maintained cordial relations with his sister, Elisabeth Forster-Nietzsche. In a speech given in 1924 at the Nietzsche Archive in Weimar, Spengler expressed sympathy with Nietzsche's tastes in art and music but complained that Nietzsche "misstated the antithesis of Christian and master-morality." Oswald Spengler, "Nietzsche and His Century," in *Selected Essays,* pg. 195.

36. Spengler, *Hour of Decision,* pg. 13.

37. Jesus's teachings were entirely about another world and have nothing do with bringing justice or peace to this one. "Give unto Caesar the things that are Caesar's" means: "Fit yourselves to the powers of the fact-world, be patient, suffer, and ask it not whether they are 'just.'" Spengler, *Decline of the West* 2:218. "Jesus was no moralizer. To see ethics as the ultimate purpose of religion is to misunderstand it. . . . A truly religious soul ignores all social issues." Spengler, *Aphorisms,* pg. 29.

38. Spengler's attacks on Catholic clergy prompted a sharp letter from the bishop of Regensburg, Rudolf Graber, in 1933. See Spengler, *Spengler Letters: 1913–1936,* pg. 292.

39. "The real Russian is a disciple of Dostoevsky." "Tolstoy's Christianity was a misunderstanding. He spoke of Christ and he meant Marx. But to Dostoevsky's Christianity the next thousand years will belong." Spengler, *Decline of the West,* 2:196. Spengler therefore recognized the possibility of a non-Western "Christianity," whose practice and doctrines would reflect a uniquely different cultural configuration. But any similarity would be semantic: the name might be the same, but the religion would be different. Russian Christianity, he argued in a 1922 speech, is an expression of a nomadic people's "mystical longing for Jerusalem and Byzantium." Oswald Spengler, "Two Faces of Russia," in *Selected Essays,* pg. 158.

40. "The unassailable privileges of the white races have been thrown away, squandered, betrayed. The adversaries have caught up with their instructors. . . . Where there is coal, or oil, or water power, there a new weapon can be forged against the heart of Faustian civilization." Oswald Spengler, *Man and Technics: A Contribution to a Philosophy of Life,* trans. Charles Francis Atkinson (New York: Alfred A. Knopf, 1932), pg. 101.

41. Oswald Spengler, "Is World Peace Possible?," in *Selected Essays,* pg. 207.

42. Spengler, *Hour of Decision,* pg. 218.

43. Spengler, *Decline of the West,* 2:131. See also Struve, *Elites Against Democracy,* pp. 232–274.

44. Spengler's rejection of racial science was attacked by leading Nazi theorist Johann von Leers in *Spenglers weltpolitisches System under der Nationalsozialistiche* (Berlin: Junker und Dünnhaupt, 1934). For an overview, see Carl Dreher, "Spengler and the Third Reich," *Virginia Quarterly Review: A National Journal of Literature and Discussion* 15, no. 2 (1939): 176–193.

45. He reached for unhelpful metaphors: "A race has roots. Race and landscape belong together. Where a plant takes root, there it dies also. There is certainly a sense in which we can, without absurdity, work backwards from a race to its 'home,' but it is much more important to realize that the race adheres permanently to this home with some of its most essential characters of body and soul. . . . A race does not migrate. Men migrate, and their successive generations are born in ever-changing landscapes; but the landscape exercises a secret force upon the plant-nature in them, and eventually the race-expression is completely transformed by the extinction of the old and the appearance of a new one." Spengler, *Decline of the West,* 2:119.

CHAPTER 2. THE FANTASIST

1. Evola's "Autodifesa" can be found as an appendix in Julius Evola, *Men Among the Ruins: Post-war Reflections of a Radical Traditionalist,* trans. Guido Stucco, ed. Michael Moynihan (Rochester, VT: Inner Traditions, 2002), pp. 287–297.

2. Julius Evola, "Guidelines," in *A Handbook for Right-Wing Youth* (London: Arktos, 2017), pp. 4–30. In his correspondence with Ernst Jünger, Carl Schmitt noted a visit by the "strange" and "much known and discussed" "Baron Evola." See Ernst Jünger and Carl Schmitt, *Ernst Jünger, Carl Schmitt: Briefe 1930–1983,* ed. Helmuth Kiesel (Stuttgart: Klett-Cotta, 1999), pg. 72.

3. Julius Evola, *The Path of Cinnabar: An Intellectual Autobiography,* trans. Sergio Knipe (London: Integral Tradition, 2009), pg. 183.

4. Paul Furlong, *Social and Political Thought of Julius Evola* (New York: Routledge, 2011), pg. 16. For surveys of Evola's role in postwar neo-fascism, see Franco Ferraresi, *Threats to Democracy: The Radical Right in Italy After the War* (Princeton, NJ: Princeton University Press, 1996), pp. 43–49; and A. James Gregor, *The Search for Neofascism: The Use and Abuse of Social Science* (New York: Cambridge, 2006), pp. 83–110.

5. Academic studies of Evola include Paul Furlong, *Julius Evola;* Francesco Cassata, *A destra del fascismo: Profilo politico di Julius Evola* (Turin: Bollati Boringhieri, 2003); and Christophe Boutin, *Politique et tradition: Julius Evola dans le siècle, 1898–1974* (Paris: Éditions Kimé, 1992).

6. Evola, *Path of Cinnabar,* pg. 20. On Evola's Dada period, see Richard Sheppard, "Julius Evola, Futurism and Dada: A Case of Double Misunderstanding," in *New Studies in Dada* (Driffield, UK: Hutton Press, 1981).

7. Julius Evola, *The Doctrine of Awakening: The Attainment of Self-Mastery According to the Earliest Buddhist Texts,* trans. H. E. Musson (Rochester, VT: Inner Traditions, 1996), pg. 35.

8. Julius Evola, *Teoria dell' individuo assoluto* (Turin: Bocca, 1927); *Fenomenologia dell'individuo assoluto* (Milan: Bocca, 1930). Evola provides detailed commentary on both books in *Path of Cinnabar,* pp. 26–66.

9. Julius Evola, "The Nature of Initiatic Knowledge," in *Introduction to Magic,* trans. Guido Stucco (Rochester, VT: Inner Traditions, 2001), pp. 26–34. "The knowledge acquired in this way cannot possibly be within everyone's reach, nor can it be transmitted to everyone without thereby degrading and desecrating it" (pg. 29). "Evola posits a new dialect of the absolute concrete individual as freedom and will, one who makes the world be by constantly surpassing it in acts of free self-creation, which at one and the same time liberate the self and dominate the world." Thomas Sheehan, "*Diventare Dio:* Julius Evola and the Metaphysics of Fascism," in *Nietzsche in Italy,* ed. Thomas Harrison (Palo Alto, CA: Stanford University Press, 1988), pg. 282.

10. Guénon saw human history as the fated process by which knowledge of a "primordial spirituality" becomes gradually more and more obscured, until it is lost and the cycle begins again. The Hindu doctrine of four ages corresponds, he argued, to what traditions in the West called Golden, Silver, Bronze, and Iron Ages. René Guénon, *The Crisis of the Modern World,* trans. Marco Pallis (Hillsdale: Sophia Perennis, 2001), pp. 6–7.

11. Julius Evola, *Revolt Against the Modern World,* trans. Guido Stucco (Rochester, VT: Inner Traditions, 1995), pg. 359.

12. See Julius Evola, *The Mystery of the Grail: Initiation and Magi in the Quest for the Spirit,* trans. Guido Stucco (Rochester, VT: Inner Traditions, 1994) and *The Hermetic Tradition: Symbols and Teachings of the Royal Art,* trans. E. Rehmus (Rochester, VT: Inner Traditions, 1995). Evola read such texts not as heterodox contributions to science or history, but as spiritual manuals that encoded their political teachings in esoteric concepts. A key feature was that their meanings are disclosed only to those initiated into a "magical-symbolic perception of the world," and cannot therefore be understood by modern "democratic" methods of study. Julius Evola, *The Yoga of Power: Tantra, Shakti, and the Secret Way,* trans. Guido Stucco (Rochester, VT: Inner Traditions, 1992), pg. 101.

13. Evola, *Path of Cinnabar,* pg. 204. Although Evola disliked being called the "Italian Spengler," he cited Spengler frequently, praising him for rejecting a progressive view of linear history, but criticizing his interpretations of Eastern religion and myth.

14. Evola, *The Hermetic Tradition,* pg. 15.

15. Julius Evola, "The Civilization of Space and the Civilization of Time," in *The Bow and the Club,* trans. Sergio Knipe (London: Arktos, 2018), pg. 4. "It is the task of Tradition to create solid riverbeds, so that the chaotic currents of life may flow in the right direction." Evola, *Revolt,* pg. 153.

16. Evola, *Revolt,* pg. 6.

17. Evola, *Path of Cinnabar,* pg. 138.

18. Evola, *Path of Cinnabar,* pg. 187.

19. Evola, *Yoga of Power,* pg. 15.

20. Evola, *Revolt,* pg. 59.

21. Evola, "American 'Civilization,'" *Scorpion,* no. 7 (1984): pp. 17–19. A democratic regime, Evola observed in 1933, begins by acknowledging the "blind should be guided by those who can see," but inevitably ends up "demanding that the blind decide who can see and who cannot." Julius Evola, *Pagan Imperialism,* trans. Cologero Salvo (Middletown: Gornahoor Press, 2018), pg. 57. This translation is based on the book's revised edition, published in German in 1932.

22. Evola, *Pagan Imperialism,* pg. 56.

23. Evola, *Path of Cinnabar,* pg. 81.

24. The statement comes from Evola's editorial in the inaugural issue of *La torre* in 1930, which was closed by Fascist authorities after five months. Evola reflects on the magazine at *Path of Cinnabar,* pg. 110.

25. Julius Evola, *Sintesi di dottrina della razza* (Milan: Hoeple, 1941). Evola provides extensive summary and commentary at *Path of Cinnabar,* pp. 164–180.

26. Julius Evola, *The Myth of the Blood: The Genesis of Racialism,* trans. John Bruce Leonard (London: Arktos, 2018).

27. "It was not Fascism that negatively affected the Italian people, the 'Italian race,' but vice versa. It was this people, this 'race' that negatively affected Fascism." Julius Evola, *Fascism Viewed from the Right,* trans. E. Christian Kopff (London: Arktos, 2018), pg. 103.

28. "Prussia had been the creation of a dynasty that had the nobility, the army, and the higher bureaucracy for its backbone. The primary element was not the 'nation' or the '*Volk*.' Rather the state, more than the land or the *ethnos,* constituted the real foundation and unifying principle. There was none of that in Hitlerism." Julius Evola, *Notes on the Third Reich,* trans. E. Christian Kopff (London: Arktos, 2013), pg. 37.

29. See Franco Ferraresi, "Julius Evola: Tradition, Reaction, and the Radical Right," *European Journal of Sociology* 28, no. 1 (1987): 107–151.

30. "The error of some extreme 'racists' who believe that the return of a race to its ethnic purity ipso facto equals its rebirth as a people consists of exactly this: they treat the human being as if he were a purebred cat, horse, or dog." Quoted in H. T. Hansen, introduction to Evola, *Men Among the Ruins,* pg. 72.

31. Cited in Evola, *Third Reich,* pg. 9. On Evola and Nazi occultism, see Nicholas Goodrick-Clarke, *Black Sun: Aryan Cults, Esoteric Nazism, and the Politics of Identity* (New York: NYU Press, 2002), pp. 52–72.

32. Evola, *Men Among the Ruins,* pg. 114.

33. Evola, "Guidelines," pg. 13. "The great illusion of our days is that democracy and liberalism are the antitheses of Communism. . . . This illusion is like saying that dusk is the antithesis of light" (pg. 11). Evola's 1929 article "Americanismo e bolscevismo" later became the final chapter of *Revolt Against the Modern World.* See Evola, *Revolt,* pp. 345–357.

34. Evola, *Men Among the Ruins,* pg. 142.

35. Paul Furlong helpfully notes that Evola's term "*l'uomo differenziato*" does not simply mean "the man who is different" but "the man who has become different." Furlong, *Julius Evola,* pg. 10.

36. Evola, *Path of Cinnabar,* pg. 198.

37. Julius Evola, *Ride the Tiger: A Survival Manual for Aristocrats of the Soul,* trans. Joscelyn Godwin and Constance Fontana (Rochester, VT: Inner Traditions, 2003).

38. Evola, *Ride the Tiger,* pg. 6.

39. Evola, *Ride the Tiger,* pg. 7. Reviewing the testimony of a former disciple of Evola, Richard Drake concludes that "all along Evola, in his private audiences with right-wing youths, freely advocated violence without truce." Richard Drake, *The Revolutionary Mystique and Terrorism in Contemporary Italy* (Bloomington: Indiana University Press, 1989), pg. 132.

40. Cited in Evola, *Path of Cinnabar,* pg. 245.

41. Evola, *Hermetic Tradition,* pg. 73. Christian spirituality prevents believers from attaining the "highest apex" of self-affirmation. Evola, *Doctrine of Awakening,* pg. 11.

42. Evola, *Path of Cinnabar,* pg. 133.

43. Evola, *Revolt,* pg. 70. "Such a split marks the beginning of the descent of civilizations in the direction that has led to the genesis of the modern world" (pg. 65).

44. For his most thoughtful discussion of Catholicism and its contest with empire in the West, see Evola, *Men Among the Ruins,* pp. 204–216, where he also laments the modern church's growing approval of liberal democracy and its defense of natural rights.

45. "An Empire which is truly an Empire cannot tolerate a Church as a distinct organization." Evola, *Pagan Imperialism,* pg. 32.

46. Evola's preface can be found at Julius Evola, "Preface to 'The Protocols of the Elders of Zion,'" Hercolano2 (blog), March 23, 2010, accessed September 12, 2018, http://hercolano2.blogspot.com/2010/03/julius-evola-preface-to-protocols-of.html. See also Julius Evola, *Three Aspects of the Jewish Problem* (Conway: Thompkins and Cariou, 2003).

47. Giorgio Almirante quotation cited in Richard Drake, "Julius Evola and the Ideological Origins of the Radical Right in Contemporary Italy" in *Political Violence and Terror: Motifs and Motivations,* ed. Peter H. Merkl (Berkeley, Los Angeles, and London: University of California Press, 1986), pg. 72.

48. As also observed by Thomas Sheehan, "Italy: Terror on the Right," *New York Review of Books,* January 22, 1981.

CHAPTER 3. THE ANTI-SEMITE

1. See "Mystery Surrounds Man Seized with Fake Passports," *Oakland Tribune,* June 9, 1960; and "Passports Jail Mystery Visitor," *San Francisco Examiner,* June 9, 1960. For details of Yockey's last days, including a review of local and national news reports, see Kevin Coogan, *Dreamer of the Day: Francis Parker Yockey and the Postwar Fascist International* (New York: Autonomedia, 1999), pp. 20–39; and Kerry Bolton, *Yockey: A Fascist Odyssey* (London: Arktos, 2018), pp. 362 ff. While I have read and closely studied Yockey's large FBI file, I am indebted to these two very different attempts to assemble its details into a chronological narrative.

2. On Carto's role in postwar conservatism and his "mentorship" by Yockey, see George Michael, *Willis Carto and the American Far Right* (Gainesville: University of Florida Press, 2008), pp. 75–87; and Leonard Zeskind, *Blood and Politics: The History of the White Nationalist Movement from the Margins to the Mainstream* (New York: Farrar, Straus and Giroux, 2009), pp. 8–16.

3. For Yockey's early life and family background, see Bolton, *Yockey,* pp. 8–23. Bolton's book is less a traditional biography than a narrative compilation of documents and personal recollections of Yockey's friends, contacts, and colleagues.

4. Francis Parker Yockey [Ulick Varange, pseud.], *Imperium,* 2 vols. (London: Westropa Press, 1948). Hereafter I will cite its author as Yockey. On the possible meanings of Yockey's pen-name, see Coogan, *Dreamer of the Day,* pg. 16; and Bolton, *Yockey,* pg. 96.

5. "The proud Civilization which in 1900 was master of 18/20ths of the earth's surface, arrived at the point in 1945, after the suicidal Second World War, where it controlled no part whatever of the earth." Yockey, *Imperium,* 1:69.

6. "This propaganda announced that 6,000,000 members of the Jewish culture-nation-state-church-people-race had been killed in European camps." Yockey, *Imperium* 2:181. Deborah Lipstadt argues that Yockey was therefore one of the first to lay the groundwork for Holocaust denial. Deborah Lipstadt, *Denying the Holocaust: The Growing Assault on Truth and Memory* (New York: Penguin, 1993), pp. 147–148.

7. See Yockey, *Imperium,* 1:73. "About the word 'Fascism' I should like to say this: I, no more than you, am not particularly attached to the word. I prefer the word Imperialism. This word has the strongest possible organic roots, is a synonym for organic health, and describes alone the entire tendency of our Cultural stage. . . . The word fascism is simply a tactical handicap for us. Imperialism is not: the Marxists have never been able to take the magic, the pride and the strength out of this fundamental word." Quoted in Bolton, *Yockey,* pg. 551.

8. See, for example, Sebastian Linderhof, "Concealed Influence: Francis Parker Yockey's Plagiarism of Carl Schmitt," *Occidental Quarterly* 10, no. 4 (Winter 2010–2011): pp. 19–62.

9. Yockey, *Imperium* 1:96.

10. Julius Evola, "On the Spiritual and Structural Prerequisites for European Unity," *Europa nazione,* 1951. Evola's comments on "Varange" reappeared in *Men Among the Ruins,* pp. 274 ff.

11. Yockey, *Imperium,* 1:18.

12. Yockey, *Imperium,* 1:67.

13. Yockey, *Imperium,* 1:279. "In high history, men risk all and die for an Idea" (pg. 48).

14. See Yockey, *Imperium,* 2:5–12.

15. "Western civilization is the site of the strongest brains and characters, the most intense moral force, the highest technical creativeness, the only positive high destiny in the world." Yockey, *Imperium,* 2:10.

16. "The culture-bearing stratum is the custodian of expression-forms of the culture. To it belong all the creators in the domains of religion, philosophy, science, music, literature, the arts of form, mathematics, politics, technics, and war, as well as the non-creators who fully understand and themselves experience the developments in this higher world, the appreciators." Yockey, *Imperium,* 1:282.

17. On Yockey's difficult relationship with Mosley and his movement, see Bolton, *Yockey,* pp. 91–104.

18. Yockey, *Imperium,* 1:328.

19. Yockey, *Imperium,* 2:41–50.

20. Yockey, *Imperium,* 2:160–172.

21. See Yockey, *Imperium,* 1:87–108.

22. Yockey, *Imperium,* 1:75.

23. See Federal Bureau of Investigation, file on Francis Parker Yockey, file #105–8229.

24. Yockey, *Imperium,* 2:58.

25. Yockey, *Imperium,* 2:70. "[T]he war between the Western culture and the Jew was a subterranean one. The Jew could not emerge in his unity and fight the West openly. . . . He favored always the side pointing towards materialism, triumph of economics, opposition to absolutism, opposition to the religious unity of the West, freedom of trade and usury" (pg. 60).

26. Quoted in Samuel Moyn, "The Alt Right's Favorite Meme Is 100 Years Old," *New York Times,* November 13, 2018.

27. On this group and their relationship with Willis Carto, see "NYA: Alive & Well Here," *Washington Post,* December 22, 1969. Two years later, they received an eleven-page story in a national magazine that discussed their Yockeyean roots at length. C. H. Simonds, "The Strange Story of Willis Carto," *National Review,* September 10, 1971, pp. 978–989. For a survey of the uses of "cultural Marxism" in contemporary discourse, see Samuel Moyn, "The Alt Right's Favorite Meme Is 100 Years Old."

28. With the exception of *Imperium,* Yockey's writings have publication histories and formats that make standard citation difficult. For the sake of convenience, I will refer to their publication in the three-volume collection of Yockey's writings recently published in the United States. *The Proclamation of London* and *The Enemy of Europe* both appear in Francis Parker Yockey, *The World in Flames: The Shorter Writings of Francis Parker Yockey,* ed. Kerry Bolton and John Morgan (n.p.: Centennial Edition Publishing, 2020).

29. Yockey's FBI file is unclear. He traveled to the Middle East possibly as early as 1951 and certainly in 1953. See #105–8229. For more detailed speculation, see Bolton, *Yockey,* pg. 217.

30. Kevin Coogan's sources place Yockey in the Prague courtroom. See *Dreamer of the Day,* pp. 264–265.

31. Francis Parker Yockey, "What Is Behind the Hanging of the Eleven Jews in Prague?," in *The World in Flames,* pp. 252–263. On the background and legacy of this bizarre essay, see Bolton, *Yockey,* pp. 307–316.

32. "Reds, Nazis Renew Act," *Washington Post,* March 31, 1954. Edmund Taylor, "Germany: Where Fascism and Communism Meet," *Reporter,* April 13, 1954, pp. 10–16. Yockey's speech for McCarthy was never delivered.

33. "The radical right's current fixation with Russia has roots, albeit slender ones, that go back more than half a century. In 1948, an American ideologue named Francis Parker Yockey wrote a book promoting pan-European fascism that saw the Soviet Union as less of a threat to Europe than the United States was. By the late 1950s, Yockey was suggesting the USSR could help 'free' Europe from U.S. domination." Mark Potok, "To Russia with Love: Why Southern U.S. Extremists Are Mad About Vladimir Putin," *Daily Beast,* August 22, 2018. See also Anton Shekhovtsov, *Russia and the Western Far Right* (New York: Routledge, 2018), pp. 18–24.

34. Yockey, *Imperium,* 1:231.

35. Coogan, *Dreamer of the Day,* pg. 184.

36. One possibility is that Yockey attempted to broker contacts between the Cuban military and former Nazi scientists. For informed speculation, see Coogan, *Dreamer of the Day,* pg. 452; and Bolton, *Yockey,* pp. 223–225.

37. Yockey, *Imperium,* 2:246. American life "is an escape from hardness into softness, from masculinity into femininity, from history to herd-grazing."

38. Francis Parker Yockey, "The World in Flames: An Estimate of the World Situation," in *The World in Flames,* pp. 397–415.

39. According to Coogan, *Dreamer of the Day,* pg. 532.

40. "Power will never stay in the hands of him who does not want power and has no plan for its use." Yockey, "World in Flames," pg. 398.

41. See Michael, *Willis Carto,* pp. 75–87.

42. Quoted in Coogan, *Dreamer of the Day,* pg. 208.

CHAPTER 4. THE PAGAN

1. Alain de Benoist, *Mémoire vive* (Paris: Éditions de Fallois, 2012), pg. 64.

2. For a reflection on a visit to America, see Alain de Benoist [Fabrice Laroche, pseud.], "Je reviens d'Amérique,"' *Europe-Action,* no. 34 (1965): pp. 9–12.

3. "I accepted the idea that race was a key factor in universal history." Benoist, *Mémoire vive,* pg. 79.

4. On the history of GRECE, see Tamir Bar-On, *Where Have All the Fascists Gone?* (New York: Ashgate, 2007); and Allen Douglas, "'La Nouvelle Droite': GRECE and the Revival of Radical Rightist Thought in Contemporary France," *Tocqueville Review* 6, no. 2 (1984): pp. 361–387. For scholarly accounts by movement sympathizers, see Michael O'Meara, *New Culture, New Right: Anti-liberalism in Postmodern Europe* (Bloomington, IN: 1st Books, 2004) and Tomislav Sunic, *Against Democracy and Equality: The European New Right* (New York: Peter Lang, 1990).

5. Alain de Benoist, *View from the Right,* vol. 1, *Heritage and Foundations,* trans. Robert Lindgren (London: Arktos, 2017); vol. 2, *Systems and Debates,* trans. Roger Adwan (London: Arktos, 2018); vol. 3, *Viewpoints and Controversies,* trans. Roger Adwan (London: Arktos, 2019).

6. Alain de Benoist, "Den alten Volksgeist erwecken," interview, *Spiegel,* August 20, 1979, pg. 159.

7. Benoist, *View from the Right,* 1:xxv, xi.

8. Benoist, *Mémoire vive,* pg. 103.

9. Alain de Benoist, "Fondements nominalistes d'une attitude devant la vie," in *Les idées à l'endroit* (Paris: Éditions Libre Hallier, 1979), pg. 34.

10. Alain de Benoist and Jean-Luc Marion, *Avec ou sans Dieu?* (Paris: Beauchesne, 1970), pg. 64.

11. Alain de Benoist, *On Being a Pagan,* trans. John Graham (Atlanta: Ultra, 2004), pg. 16. Benoist's anti-Christian writings are extensive. See also, for example, "Le bolshevisme de l'antiquité," in *Les idées à l'endroit;* "Der Konflikt der antiken Kultur mit dem Urchristentum," in Pierre Krebs, ed., *Das unvergängliche Erbe: Alternativen zum Prinzip der Gleichheit* (Tübingen: Grabert Verlag, 1981); and "Monotheism versus Polytheism," *Chronicles,* March 1, 1996.

12. "The Christian religion proclaims, in effect, the unique value of every human being by positing him as a value in himself. Insofar as he possesses a soul which puts him in a direct relationship with God, man becomes the bearer of an absolute value, that is to say, of a value which cannot be confused either with his personal qualities or with his belonging to a particular collective group." Alain de Benoist, *Beyond Human Rights: Defending Freedoms,* trans. Alexander Jacob (London: Arktos, 2011), pg. 27.

13. Benoist, *Beyond Human Rights,* pg. 39.

14. See Richard Wolin, *The Seduction of Unreason: The Intellectual Romance with Fascism from Nietzsche to Postmodernism* (Princeton, NJ: Princeton University Press, 2004), pp. 256 ff.

15. Alain de Benoist, *The Problem of Democracy,* trans. Sergio Knipe (London: Arktos, 2011).

16. Benoist, *The Problem of Democracy,* pg. 23. "In Greek democracy, the individual did not have direct access to political life: he participated in public life as a member of a genos, of a family or a clan." Alain de Benoist, "The First Federalist: Johannes Althusius," in *Democracy and Populism: The Telos Essays,* ed. Russell A. Berman and Timothy W. Luke (Candor, NY: Telos Press, 2018), pg. 130.

17. Benoist, *The Problem of Democracy,* pp. 24, 28, 41. "Each national culture has a principle of legitimacy of its own, a specific mission entrusted to its own leaders in accordance with its own history and personality" (pg. 42). Cf. Carl Schmitt, *The Crisis of Parliamentary Democracy,* trans. Ellen Kennedy (Cambridge,

MA: MIT Press, 1985), pg. 9. Benoist's argument against liberal democracy and his concern for "homogeneity" echo Schmitt's 1923 book.

18. On his understanding of social symbiosis, see Benoist, "First Federalist," pg. 130.

19. Alain de Benoist, *Europe, Tiers monde, même combat* (Paris: Robert Laffont, 1986).

20. Alain de Benoist, "The Current Crisis of Democracy," in *Democracy and Populism*, pg. 292.

21. See Alain de Benoist, "Wider den Individualismus," in *Die entscheidenden Jahre* (Tübingen: Grabert Verglag, 1982).

22. Under liberalism, Benoist concludes, "[m]an is free to give the meaning that he wants to his life, but he has no markers that would allow him to give meaning to this meaning." Alain de Benoist, *Minima Moralia: Per un'etica delle virtù* (Milan: Bietti, 2017). This volume is available in French, without pagination, at https://s3-eu-west-1.amazonaws.com/alaindebenoist/pdf/minima_moralia.pdf (accessed October 2, 2020).

23. Alain de Benoist, "Critique of Liberal Ideology," trans. Greg Johnson, *Occidental Quarterly* 7, no. 4 (Winter 2007–2008): pg. 13.

24. Alain de Benoist and Charles Champetier, *Manifesto for a European Renaissance*, trans. Martin Mandelow (London: Arktos, 2012), pg. 32.

25. "[T]he European mind is above all philosophical. Philosophy can only arise where there are no definitive behaviors and solutions." Alain de Benoist, "'We Can Only Reach Universality through Particulars': The Question of the Right: The 1993 Interview," in *Democracy and Populism*, pg. 43.

26. Benoist, *View from the Right*, 1:5.

27. Benoist, "Fondements nominalistes d'une attitude devant la vie," pg. 38; Benoist and Champetier, *Manifesto*, pg. 13.

28. Benoist's argument draws from a number of different thinkers. The term "holism" is borrowed from the work of Louis Dumont. See Louis Dumont, *Essays on Individualism: Modern Ideology in Anthropological Perspective* (Chicago: University of Chicago Press, 1986).

29. Alain de Benoist, "On Identity," in *Democracy and Populism*, pg. 236.

30. See Pierre-André Taguieff, "From Race to Culture: The New Right's View of European Identity," *Telos*, no. 98–99 (1993): pp. 99–125.

31. Benoist, "On Identity," pg. 251. Identity "refers to what distinguishes—the singularity or uniqueness." Benoist, "Preface to the New Edition," *View from the Right*, 1:xv.

32. Benoist, *View from the Right*, 1:xxvii.

33. "You can have an identity without an enemy; but you can't have an identity without somebody else having another identity." Alain de Benoist, "The 'European New Right': Defining and Defending Europe's Heritage – An Interview with Alain de Benoist," interview by Donald I. Warren [pseud. Ian B. Warren], *Journal of Historical Review* 14, no. 2 (1994): pg. 32. Cf. Carl Schmitt, *The Concept of the Political,* trans. George Schwab (Chicago: University of Chicago Press, 1996), pp. 26–27.

34. Xenophobia is a "brutal repelling of the other," based on fear rather than respect. Benoist, "Universality through Particulars," pg. 42. "Whoever destroys the identity of another does not reinforce his own, but renders it more vulnerable." Benoist, *View from the Right,* 1:xxv.

35. "Although Christian love may well put the accent on the 'love of one's neighbor,' by definition it never stops at the neighbor. . . . It does not know any borders." Benoist, *Beyond Human Rights,* pg. 29. For a similar argument, from which Benoist is clearly drawing, see Carl Schmitt, *The* Nomos *of the Earth in the International Law of the* Jus Publicum Europaeum, trans. G. L. Ulmen (Candor, NY: Telos Press, 2003), pg. 104.

36. Benoist, *View from the Right,* 2:388.

37. "The pagan man experiences the place where he is born as a relation of filiation. He has his 'mother country,' while in biblical monotheism, the earth is not an original land, a homeland." Alain de Benoist, "The Religion of Europe," *Éléments,* no. 36 (1980).

38. Quoted in Pierre-André Taguieff, *Sur la Nouvelle Droite: Jalons d'une analyse critique* (Paris: Descartes & Cie, 1994), pg. 15.

39. Benoist's exchange of letters with classicist Revilo P. Oliver from 1970 to 1975 can be found at Alain de Benoist and Revilo P. Oliver, letters, 1970–1975, Revilo P. Oliver Papers, updated in 2010 (accessed March 4, 2019), http://www.revilo-oliver.com/papers/ (accessed March 4, 2019).

40. See Tamir Bar-on, *Rethinking the French New Right: Alternatives to Modernity* (New York: Routledge, 2013), pp. 10–31.

41. Alain de Benoist and Tomislav Sunic, "Gemeinschaft and Gesellschaft: A Sociological View of the Decay of Modern Society," *Mankind Quarterly* 34, no. 3 (1994): pg. 263; Benoist, *Mémoire vive,* pp. 116, 181.

42. Alain de Benoist, "What Is Racism?," *Telos,* no. 114 (1999): pg. 15.

43. Benoist, "What Is Racism?," pg. 25.

44. Quotation from a 1997 interview in Bar-On, *Where Have All the Fascists Gone?,* pg. 86.

45. See Alain de Benoist, "On Indistinction," *Occidental Quarterly* 12, no. 4 (Winter 2012–2013).

46. Benoist and Champetier, *Manifesto,* pg. 34. "Humanity is necessarily pluralistic. . . . It is comprised of different families – and does not constitute a family in itself." Benoist, *Problem of Democracy,* pg. 99. Drawing from the work of David Reich, Benoist comments: "[racial] groups are characterized by a specific common ancestry, a distinct geographical origin, genetic kinship, and visible common biological traits." Alain de Benoist, "La schizophrénie de l'antiracisme," *Éléments,* no. 145 (2018): pg. 45.

47. Benoist, "What Is Racism?," pg. 46.

48. Benoist, "La schizophrénie de l'antiracisme," pg. 45.

49. Benoist, *Mémoire vive,* pg. 174.

50. Benoist, "Universality through Particulars," pg. 37.

51. For an introduction to the movement and some of its activists, see José Pedro Zúquete, *The Identitarians: The Movement Against Globalism and Islam in Europe* (Notre Dame, IN: University of Notre Dame Press, 2018); and Thomas Chatterton Williams, "The French Origins of 'You Will Not Replace Us,'" *New Yorker,* November 27, 2017. Identitarian movements have also been influenced by a former intellectual collaborator of Benoist's, Guillaume Faye, who has pressed the founding ideas of GRECE in a much more radical direction. See, for example, Faye's recent book, published shortly after his death, *Ethnic Apocalypse: The Coming European Civil War* (London: Arktos, 2019). For one study of this issue in France, see Alberto Spektorowski, "The French New Right: Multiculturalism of the Right and the Recognition/Exclusionism Syndrome," *Journal of Global Ethics* 8, no. 1 (2012): pp. 41–61.

52. Samuel Francis, "The Real Right?," *Occidental Quarterly* 4, no. 4 (Fall 2004): pp. 68–82.

CHAPTER 5. THE NATIONALIST

1. Samuel Francis, "From Household to Nation," in *Revolution from the Middle* (Raleigh: Middle American Press, 1997), pp. 229–243. As Limbaugh summarized the essay, "The Republican Party establishment does not understand this. They do not know who their conservative voters are. They've overestimated their conservatism, and by that is meant they think they're dyed-in-the-wool conservative theoreticians absorbed in such things as the free market and all these other bells and whistles, and they're not. They're not liberal. They're not Democrat. Many of them do not want to be thought of as conservatives, for a host of reasons." My discussion of Limbaugh's program draws on a recording from his website that has since been removed, though a transcript is still available. See Rush Limbaugh, "Understanding Trump's Appeal," *Rush Limbaugh Show,* January 20, 2016, https://

www.rushlimbaugh.com/daily/2016/01/20/understanding_trump_s_appeal-2. (recording accessed August 10, 2018). Limbaugh's comments were inspired by and also drew from a column on Francis by Michael Brendan Dougherty, "How an Obscure Advisor to Pat Buchanan Predicted the Wild Trump Campaign in 1996," *Week,* January 19, 2016, https://theweek.com/articles/599577/how-obscure-adviser-pat-buchanan-predicted-wild-trump-campaign-1996.

2. For one prominent example, see David Frum, "Unpatriotic Conservatives: A War Against America," *National Review,* April 2, 2003.

3. Taylor's eulogy is reprinted in Samuel Francis, *Essential Writings on Race,* ed. Jared Taylor (Oakton, VA: New Century Books, 2007), pp. 1–3.

4. Samuel Francis, "The Buchanan Revolution," in *Revolution from the Middle,* pg. 139.

5. For information about Francis's personal life and family background, I have relied on Michael Brendan Dougherty, "The Castaway," America's Future Foundation, January 14, 2007, https://americasfuture.org/the-castaway. See also Dougherty, "Obscure Advisor." More than any other journalist, Dougherty is responsible for bringing Francis back into public discussion.

6. Samuel Francis, "Ideas and No Consequences," in *Beautiful Losers: Essays on the Failure of American Conservatism* (Columbia: University of Missouri Press, 1993), pp. 2–3.

7. Samuel Francis, "The Other Side of Modernism," in *Beautiful Losers,* pp. 129–138.

8. On Pareto's distinction between "logical" and "illogical" actions, on which Francis's distinction relies, see *Mind and Society,* trans. Arthur Livingston (New York: Harcourt Brace, 1935), pp. 151 ff. Francis was initiated into Pareto through the chapter on him in James Burnham, *The Machiavellians: Defenders of Freedom* (New York: John Day, 1943), pp. 171–222. Francis authored a short introduction to Burnham, *Power and History: The Political Thought of James Burnham* (Lanham, MD: University Press of America, 1984). It was later revised and republished as *James Burnham* (London: Claridge Press, 1999).

9. See Samuel Francis, "The Harmless Persuasion," in *Beautiful Losers,* pp. 88–94.

10. "[W]e will find little in conservative theory to instruct us in the strategy and tactics of challenging dominant authorities. Instead, we need to look to the left to understand how a politically subordinated and culturally dispossessed majority of Americans can recover its rightful position as the dominant and creative core of American society." Samuel Francis, "Winning the Culture War," in *Revolution from the Middle,* pg. 175.

11. James Burnham, *The Managerial Revolution: What Is Happening in the*

World (New York: John Day, 1941). For background, see Daniel Kelly, *James Burnham and the Struggle for the World: A Life* (Wilmington, DE: I.S.I. Books, 2002).

12. Samuel Francis, *Leviathan and Its Enemies: Mass Organization and Managerial Power in Twentieth-Century America* (Arlington, VA: Washington Summit Publishers, 2016), pg. 9. For one of the only reviews of the book in a mainstream outlet, see Timothy Shenk, "The Dark History of Donald Trump's Right-Wing Revolt," *Guardian*, August 16, 2016.

13. "The homogenization of the mass population as political participants, consumers, and audience creates a uniform collective identity susceptible to the manipulative disciplines of the mass organizations and their elites." Francis, *Leviathan*, pp. 80–81.

14. Francis, *Leviathan*, pg. 14. As he put it more colorfully elsewhere, "It tells you your heritage, your literature, your art, your holidays, your religion, your music, your beliefs, your country and your very skin color are garbage and mere tricks by which you and your class and your race have tyrannized mankind." Samuel Francis, "Revolution from the Middle," in *Revolution from the Middle*, pg. 71.

15. See Donald I. Warren, *The Radical Center: Middle Americans and the Politics of Alienation* (Notre Dame, IN: University of Notre Dame Press, 1976); "The Politics of the Displaced Majority," *Telos*, no. 95 (1993): pp. 147–160; and "White Americans as a Minority," *Telos*, no. 104 (1995): pp. 127–134. See also John Judis, "The Return of the Middle American Radical," *National Journal*, October 2, 2015.

16. Samuel Francis, "Message from MARs: The Social Politics of the New Right," in *Beautiful Losers*, pg. 62. Francis was paraphrasing Warren.

17. Francis, "Message from MARs," pg. 74.

18. Patrick J. Buchanan, foreword to Samuel Francis, *Shots Fired: Sam Francis on America's Culture War*, ed. Peter Gemma (Vienna, VA: Fitzgerald Griffin Foundation, 2006); Samuel Francis, "The Buchanan Revolution – Part Two," in *Revolution from the Middle*, pp. 140–147.

19. Bill Clinton's speech on changing racial demographics at Portland State University can be found at William Jefferson Clinton, "Remarks by the President at Portland State University Commencement," Archived Clinton White House Website – Version 4, June 13, 1998, accessed October 1, 2020, https://clintonwhitehouse4.archives.gov/textonly/WH/New/html/19980615-12352.html. His comments to a meeting of journalists at the White House were reported in a newspaper column by Patrick Buchanan; see Patrick J. Buchanan, "Who Voted for Clinton's Revolution?," Patrick J. Buchanan – Official Website, July 1, 1997, accessed October 1, 2020, https://buchanan.org/blog/pjb-who-voted-for-clintons-revolution-378.

20. Samuel Francis, "All Those Things to Apologize For," *Washington Times,* June 27, 1995. Francis's column was prompted by a resolution of the Southern Baptist Convention that apologized for slavery.

21. Samuel Francis, "Why Race Matters," in *Essential Writings on Race,* pg. 7.

22. Samuel Francis, "Ethnopolitics: Ethnic and Racial Implications of the 2000 Election," in *Essential Writings on Race,* pg. 96.

23. For a collection of his writings on immigration, see Samuel Francis, *America Extinguished: Mass Immigration and the Disintegration of American Culture* (Monterey, VA: Americans for Immigration Control, 2002).

24. See Samuel Francis, "Race and the American Identity," in *Essential Writings on Race,* pg. 60.

25. Samuel Francis, "Why Race Matters," in *Essential Writings on Race,* pg. 14.

26. Francis, "Why Race Matters," pg. 14.

27. Samuel Francis, "The Roots of the White Man," in *Essential Writings on Race,* pg. 49.

28. Francis, "Roots of the White Man," pp. 29–52.

29. Samuel Francis, "The Christian Question," in *Essential Writings on Race,* pg. 101.

30. Francis, "Winning the Culture War," pg. 175.

31. Francis, "Revolution from the Middle," pg. 87.

32. Francis, "Message from MARs," pg. 61.

33. Francis, "Revolution from the Middle," pg. 87.

CHAPTER 6. THE CHRISTIAN QUESTION

1. See George Hawley, *The Alt-Right: What Everybody Needs to Know* (New York: Oxford University Press, 2018); and Michael Anton, "Are the Kids Al(t) Right?," *Claremont Review of Books,* Summer 2019. For other recent studies of the alt-right, see Thomas Main, *The Rise of the Alt-Right* (Washington, DC: Brookings Institution Press, 2018); and Ronald Beiner, *Dangerous Minds: Nietzsche, Heidegger, and the Return of the Far Right* (Philadelphia: University of Pennsylvania Press, 2019).

2. Greg Johnson, "Interview on Christianity, Part 2" (interview with Alain de Benoist), *Counter Currents,* January 29, 2011, https://counter-currents.com/2011/01/interview-on-christianity-part-2/; Richard Spencer, *Radix Podcast, Radix Journal,* https://radixjournal.com/podcasts/; Kevin MacDonald, "Christianity and the Ethnic Suicide of the West," *Occidental Observer,* April 27, 2015, https://www.theoccidentalobserver.net/2015/04/27/christianity-and-the-ethnic-suicide-of-the-west/; Gregory Hood, "Why Christianity Can't Save Us," *Counter Currents,* July 31, 2013, https://counter-currents.com/2013/07/why-christianity-cant-save-us/; Arthur Kemp, *March of the Titans: The Complete History of the White Race* (Burlington, IA: Ostara Publications, 2016), pg. 530. For an influential memoir that recounts the author's loss of Christian faith and embrace of white nationalism, see William Gayley Simpson, *Which Way Western Man?* (Cooperstown, NY: Yeoman Press, 1978).

3. For a sustained interpretation of Christianity along these lines, see Marcel Gauchet, *The Disenchantment of the World: A Political History of Religion,* trans. Oscar Burge (Princeton, NJ: Princeton University Press, 1997).

4. On resistance to transcendence, see Ernst Nolte, *Three Faces of Fascism: Action Française, Italian Fascism, National Socialism,* trans. Leila Vennewitz (New York: Holt, Rinehart, and Winston, 1966), pp. 429–434.

5. On the political use of Christian identity in right-wing populism, see Nadia Marzouki, Olivier Roy, and Duncan McDonnell, eds., *Saving the People: How Populists Hijack Religion* (New York: Oxford University Press, 2016).

6. Edward J. Watts, *The Final Pagan Generation: Rome's Unexpected Path to Christianity* (Berkeley: University of California Press, 2015).

7. *Letter to Diognetus.* I have used the following translation: "From a Letter to Diognetus: The Christian in the World," Holy See (the Vatican), accessed May 3, 2020, http://www.vatican.va/spirit/documents/spirit_20010522_diogneto_en.html.

8. Galatians 3:28; Acts 17:26.

9. In this section, I have drawn from Denise Kimber Buell, *Why This New Race: Ethnic Reasoning in Early Christianity* (New York: Columbia University Press, 2005).

10. Denise Kimber Buell, *Why This New Race,* pg. 113.

11. According to Galatians 3:7, "those who have faith are children of Abraham."

12. For recent explorations of these ideas, see Yoram Hazony, *The Virtue of Nationalism* (New York: Basic Books, 2018) and R. R. Reno, *Return of the Strong Gods: Nationalism, Populism, and the Future of the West* (Washington, DC: Regnery Gateway, 2019).

13. John Paul II, *Memory and Identity: Conversations at the Dawn of a Millennium* (New York: Rizzoli, 2005), pg. 70. The pope expressed concern that Western nations were reaching an age of "post-identity" (pg. 86). The pope affirmed the church's teaching that "the divinely sanctioned natural order divides the human race into social groups, nations or States, which are mutually independent in organization and in the direction of their internal life." Pius XII, *Summi Pontificatus*, pg. 72. Pius XII, *Summi Pontificatus*, Holy See (Vatican), October 20, 1939, http://www.vatican.va/content/pius-xii/en/encyclicals/documents/hf_p-xii_enc_20101939_summi-pontificatus.html.

BIBLIOGRAPHY

Angelos, James. "The Prophet of Germany's New Right." *New York Times Magazine,* October 10, 2017.

Anton, Michael. "Are the Kids Al(t) Right?" *Claremont Review of Books,* Summer 2019.

Bar-On, Tamir. *Rethinking the French New Right: Alternatives to Modernity.* New York: Routledge, 2013.

——. *Where Have All the Fascists Gone?* New York: Ashgate, 2007.

Beauchamp, Zack. "The Anti-liberal Moment." *Vox,* September 9, 2019. https://www.vox.com/policy-and-politics/2019/9/9/20750160/liberalism-trump-putin-socialism-reactionary.

Beiner, Ronald. *Dangerous Minds: Nietzsche, Heidegger, and the Return of the Far Right.* Philadelphia: University of Pennsylvania Press, 2019.

de Benoist, Alain. "Den alten Volksgeist erwecken." Interview. *Spiegel,* August 20, 1979, 157–162.

——. *Beyond Human Rights: Defending Freedoms.* Translated by Alexander Jacob. London: Arktos, 2011.

——. "Le bolshevisme de l'antiquité." In *Les idées à l'endroit.*

——. "Critique of Liberal Ideology." Translated by Greg Johnson. *Occidental Quarterly* 7, no. 4 (Winter 2007–2008).

——. "The Current Crisis of Democracy." In *Democracy and Populism.*

——. *Democracy and Populism: The Telos Essays.* Edited by Russell A. Berman and Timothy W. Luke. Candor, NY: Telos Press, 2018.

——. *Europe, Tiers monde, même combat.* Paris: Robert Laffont, 1986.

——. "The 'European New Right': Defining and Defending Europe's Heritage – An

Interview with Alain de Benoist." By Donald I. Warren [pseud. Ian B. Warren]. *Journal of Historical Review* 14, no. 2 (1994): 28–37.
——. "The First Federalist: Johannes Althusius." In *Democracy and Populism.*
——. "Fondements nominalistes d'une attitude devant la vie." In *Les idées à l'endroit.*
——. *Les idées à l'endroit.* Paris: Éditions Libre Hallier, 1979.
——. [Fabrice Laroche, pseud.]. "Je reviens d'Amérique." *Europe-Action,* no. 34 (1965): 9–12.
——. "Der Konflikt der antiken Kultur mit dem Urchristentum." In *Das unvergängliche Erbe: Alternativen zum Prinzip der Gleichheit,* edited by Pierre Krebs. Tübingen: Grabert Verlag, 1981.
——. *Mémoire vive.* Paris: Éditions de Fallois, 2012.
——. *Minima Moralia: Per un'etica delle virtù.* Milan: Bietti, 2017. https://s3-eu-west-1.amazonaws.com/alaindebenoist/pdf/minima_moralia.pdf.
——. "Monotheism versus Polytheism." *Chronicles,* March 1, 1996.
——. *On Being a Pagan.* Translated by John Graham. Atlanta: Ultra, 2004.
——. "On Identity." In *Democracy and Populism.*
——. "On Indistinction." *Occidental Quarterly* 12, no. 4 (Winter 2012–2013).
——. *The Problem of Democracy.* Translated by Sergio Knipe. London: Arktos, 2011.
——. "The Religion of Europe." *Éléments,* no. 36 (1980).
——. "La schizophrénie de l'antiracisme." *Éléments,* no. 145 (2018).
——. *View from the Right.* Vol. 1, *Heritage and Foundations,* translated by Robert Lindgren. London: Arktos, 2017.
——. *View from the Right.* Vol. 2, *Systems and Debates,* translated by Roger Adwan. London: Arktos, 2018.
——. *View from the Right.* Vol. 3, *Viewpoints and Controversies,* translated by Roger Adwan. London: Arktos, 2019.
——. "'We Can Only Reach Universality through Particulars': The Question of the Right: The 1993 Interview." In *Democracy and Populism.*
——. "What Is Racism?" *Telos,* no. 114 (1999): 11–48.
——. "Wider den Individualismus." In *Die entscheidenden Jahre.* Tübingen: Grabert Verglag, 1982.
de Benoist, Alain, and Charles Champetier. *Manifesto for a European Renaissance.* Translated by Martin Mandelow. London: Arktos, 2012.
de Benoist, Alain, and Jean-Luc Marion. *Avec ou sans Dieu?* Paris: Beauchesne, 1970.
de Benoist, Alain, and Revilo P. Oliver. Letters. 1970–1975. Revilo P. Oliver Papers. Updated in 2010. Accessed March 4, 2019. http://www.revilo-oliver.com/papers/.
de Benoist, Alain, and Tomislav Sunic. "Gemeinschaft and Gesellschaft: A Sociological View of the Decay of Modern Society." *Mankind Quarterly* 34, no. 3 (1994): 261–270.

BIBLIOGRAPHY

Berlin, Isaiah. *The Crooked Timber of Humanity: Chapters in the History of Ideas.* 2nd ed. Edited by Henry Hardy. Princeton, NJ: Princeton University Press, 2013.

Bolton, Kerry. *Yockey: A Fascist Odyssey.* London: Arktos, 2018.

Boutin, Christophe. *Politique et tradition: Julius Evola dans le siècle, 1898–1974.* Paris: Éditions Kimé, 1992.

Buchanan, Patrick J. "Who Voted for Clinton's Revolution?" Patrick J. Buchanan–Official Website, July 1, 1997. Accessed October 1, 2020. https://buchanan.org/blog/pjb-who-voted-for-clintons-revolution-378.

Buell, Denise Kimber. *Why This New Race: Ethnic Reasoning in Early Christianity.* New York: Columbia University Press, 2005.

Burnham, James. *The Machiavellians: Defenders of Freedom.* New York: John Day, 1943.

——. *The Managerial Revolution: What Is Happening in the World.* New York: John Day, 1941.

Cassata, Francesco. *A destra del fascismo: Profilo politico di Julius Evola.* Turin: Bollati Boringhieri, 2003.

Clinton, William Jefferson. "Remarks by the President at Portland State University Commencement." Archived Clinton White House Website–Version 4. June 13, 1998. Accessed October 1, 2020. https://clintonwhitehouse4.archives.gov/textonly/WH/New/html/19980615-12352.html.

Coogan, Kevin. *Dreamer of the Day: Francis Parker Yockey and the Postwar Fascist International.* New York: Autonomedia, 1999.

Dougherty, Michael Brendan. "The Castaway." America's Future Foundation, January 14, 2007. https://americasfuture.org/the-castaway.

——. "How an Obscure Advisor to Pat Buchanan Predicted the Wild Trump Campaign in 1996." *Week,* January 19, 2016. https://theweek.com/articles/599577/how-obscure-adviser-pat-buchanan-predicted-wild-trump-campaign-1996.

Douglas, Allen. "'La Nouvelle Droite': GRECE and the Revival of Radical Rightist Thought in Contemporary France." *Tocqueville Review* 6, no. 2 (1984): 361–387.

Drake, Richard. "Julius Evola and the Ideological Origins of the Radical Right in Contemporary Italy." In *Political Violence and Terror: Motifs and Motivations,* edited by Peter H. Merkl. Berkeley, Los Angeles, and London: University of California Press, 1986.

——. *The Revolutionary Mystique and Terrorism in Contemporary Italy.* Bloomington: Indiana University Press, 1989.

Dreher, Carl. "Spengler and the Third Reich." *Virginia Quarterly Review: A National Journal of Literature and Discussion* 15, no. 2 (1939): 176–193.

Duchesne, Ricardo. *Faustian Man and Multicultural Society.* London: Arktos, 2017.

Dumont, Louis. *Essays on Individualism: Modern Ideology in Anthropological Perspective.* Chicago: University of Chicago Press, 1986.

BIBLIOGRAPHY

Evola, Julius. "American 'Civilization.'" *Scorpion*, no. 7 (1984): 17–19.

——. "Autodifesa." In *Men Among the Ruins*.

——. "The Civilization of Space and the Civilization of Time." In *The Bow and the Club*. Translated by Sergio Knipe. London: Arktos, 2018.

——. *The Doctrine of Awakening: The Attainment of Self-Mastery According to the Earliest Buddhist Texts*. Translated by H. E. Musson. Rochester, VT: Inner Traditions, 1996.

——. *Fascism Viewed from the Right*. Translated by E. Christian Kopff. London: Arktos, 2018.

——. *Fenomenologia dell'individuo assoluto*. Milan: Bocca, 1930.

——. "Guidelines." In *A Handbook for Right-Wing Youth*. London: Arktos, 2017.

——. *The Hermetic Tradition: Symbols and Teachings of the Royal Art*. Translated by E. Rehmus. Rochester, VT: Inner Traditions, 1995.

——. *Men Among the Ruins: Post-War Reflections of a Radical Traditionalist*. With an introduction by H. T. Hansen. Edited by Michael Moynihan. Translated by Guido Stucco. Rochester, VT: Inner Traditions, 2002.

——. *The Mystery of the Grail: Initiation and Magi in the Quest for the* Spirit. Translated by Guido Stucco. Rochester, VT: Inner Traditions, 1994.

——. "The Nature of Initiatic Knowledge." In *Introduction to Magic*. Translated by Guido Stucco. Rochester, VT: Inner Traditions, 2001.

——. *Notes on the Third Reich*. Translated by E. Christian Kopff. London: Arktos, 2013.

——. "On the Spiritual and Structural Prerequisites for European Unity." *Europa nazione*, 1951.

——. *Pagan Imperialism*. Translated by Cologero Salvo. Middletown: Gornahoor Press, 2018.

——. *The Path of Cinnabar: An Intellectual Autobiography*. Translated by Sergio Knipe. London: Integral Tradition, 2009.

——. "Preface to 'The Protocols of the Elders of Zion.'" *Hercolano2* (blog). March 23, 2010. Accessed September 12, 2018. http://hercolano2.blogspot.com/2010/03/julius-evola-preface-to-protocols-of.html.

——. *Revolt Against the Modern World*. Translated by Guido Stucco. Rochester, VT: Inner Traditions, 1995.

——. *Ride the Tiger: A Survival Manual for Aristocrats of the Soul*. Translated by Joscelyn Godwin and Constance Fontana. Rochester, VT: Inner Traditions, 2003.

——. *Sintesi di dottrina della razza*. Milan: Hoeple, 1941.

——. *Teoria dell' individuo assoluto*. Turin: Bocca, 1927.

——. *Three Aspects of the Jewish Problem*. Conway: Thompkins and Cariou, 2003.

——. *The Yoga of Power: Tantra, Shakti, and the Secret Way.* Translated by Guido Stucco. Rochester, VT: Inner Traditions, 1992.

Farrenkopf, John. *Prophet of Decline: Spengler on World History and Politics.* Baton Rouge: Louisiana State University Press, 2001.

Faye, Guillaume. *Ethnic Apocalypse: The Coming European Civil War.* London: Arktos, 2019.

Federal Bureau of Investigation. File on Francis Parker Yockey. File #105-8229.

Ferraresi, Franco. "Julius Evola: Tradition, Reaction, and the Radical Right." *European Journal of Sociology* 28, no. 1 (1987): 107–151.

——. *Threats to Democracy: The Radical Right in Italy after the War.* Princeton, NJ: Princeton University Press, 1996.

Francis, Samuel. "All Those Things to Apologize For." *Washington Times,* June 27, 1995.

——. *America Extinguished: Mass Immigration and the Disintegration of American Culture.* Monterey, VA: Americans for Immigration Control, 2002.

——. *Beautiful Losers: Essays on the Failure of American Conservatism.* Columbia: University of Missouri Press, 1993.

——. "The Buchanan Revolution." In *Revolution from the Middle.*

——. "The Buchanan Revolution – Part Two." In *Revolution from the Middle.*

——. "The Christian Question." In *Essential Writings on Race.*

——. *Essential Writings on Race.* Edited with an introduction by Jared Taylor. Oakton, VA: New Century Books, 2007.

——. "Ethnopolitics: Ethnic and Racial Implications of the 2000 Election." In *Essential Writings on Race.*

——. "From Household to Nation." In *Revolution from the Middle.*

——. "The Harmless Persuasion." In *Beautiful Losers.*

——. "Ideas and No Consequences." In *Beautiful Losers.*

——. *James Burnham.* London: Claridge Press, 1999.

——. *Leviathan and Its Enemies: Mass Organization and Managerial Power in Twentieth-Century America.* Arlington, VA: Washington Summit Publishers, 2016.

——. "Message from MARs: The Social Politics of the New Right." In *Beautiful Losers.*

——. "The Other Side of Modernism." In *Beautiful Losers.*

——. *Power and History: The Political Thought of James Burnham.* Lanham, MD: University Press of America, 1984.

——. "Race and the American Identity." In *Essential Writings on Race.*

——. "The Real Right?" *Occidental Quarterly* 4, no. 4 (Fall 2004): pp. 68–82.

——. *Revolution from the Middle.* Raleigh, NC: Middle American Press, 1997.

——. "Revolution from the Middle." In *Revolution from the Middle.*

——. "The Roots of the White Man." In *Essential Writings on Race.*

——. *Shots Fired: Sam Francis on America's Culture War.* Edited by Peter Gemma, with a foreword by Patrick J. Buchanan. Vienna, VA: Fitzgerald Griffin Foundation, 2006.

——. "Why Race Matters." In *Essential Writings on Race.*

——. "Winning the Culture War." In *Revolution from the Middle.*

Friedell, Egon. *A Cultural History of the Modern Age: Renaissance and Reformation.* New York: Routledge, 2017.

"From a Letter to Diognetus: The Christian in the World." Holy See (Vatican). Accessed May 3, 2020. http://www.vatican.va/spirit/documents/spirit_20010522_diogneto_en.html.

Frum, David. "Unpatriotic Conservatives: A War Against America." *National Review,* April 2, 2003.

Frye, Northrop. "The Decline of the West." *Daedalus* 103, no. 1 (1974): 1–13.

Furlong, Paul. *Social and Political Thought of Julius Evola.* New York: Routledge, 2011.

Gauchet, Marcel. *The Disenchantment of the World: A Political History of Religion.* Translated by Oscar Burge. Princeton, NJ: Princeton University Press, 1997.

Goodrick-Clarke, Nicholas. *Black Sun: Aryan Cults, Esoteric Nazism, and the Politics of Identity.* New York: NYU Press, 2002.

Gregor, A. James. *The Search for Neofascism: The Use and Abuse of Social Science.* New York: Cambridge, 2006.

Guénon, René. *The Crisis of the Modern World.* Translated by Marco Pallis. Hillsdale: Sophia Perennis, 2001.

Hawley, George. *The Alt-Right: What Everybody Needs to Know.* New York: Oxford University Press, 2018.

——. *Making Sense of the Alt-Right.* New York: Columbia University Press, 2017.

Hazony, Yoram. *The Virtue of Nationalism.* New York: Basic Books, 2018.

Heidegger, Martin. *Off the Beaten Path.* Translated by Julian Young. New York: Cambridge University Press, 2002.

Heller, Erich. *The Disinherited Mind: Essays in Modern German Literature and Thought.* Orlando, FL: Harcourt Brace, 1975.

Herf, Jeffrey. *Reactionary Modernism: Technology, Politics and Culture in Weimar and the Third Reich.* New York: Cambridge University Press, 1984.

Hood, Gregory. "Why Christianity Can't Save Us." *Counter Currents,* July 31, 2013. https://counter-currents.com/2013/07/why-christianity-cant-save-us/.

John Paul II. *Memory and Identity: Conversations at the Dawn of a Millennium.* New York: Rizzoli, 2005.

Johnson, Greg. "Interview on Christianity, Part 2." Interview with Alain de Benoist. *Counter-Currents,* January 29, 2011. https://counter-currents.com/2011/01/interview-on-christianity-part-2/.

Judis, John. "The Return of the Middle American Radical." *National Journal,* October 2, 2015.

Jünger, Ernst, and Carl Schmitt. *Ernst Jünger, Carl Schmitt: Briefe 1930–1983.* Edited by Helmuth Kiesel. Stuttgart: Klett-Cotta, 1999.

Kaufmann, Eric. *Whiteshift: Populism, Immigration, and the Future of White Majorities.* New York: Abrams Press, 2019.

Kelly, Daniel. *James Burnham and the Struggle for the World: A Life.* Wilmington, DE: I.S.I. Books, 2002.

Kemp, Arthur. *March of the Titans: The Complete History of the White Race.* Burlington, IA: Ostara Publications, 2016.

Kojève, Alexandre. *Introduction to the Reading of Hegel.* Compiled by Raymond Queneau. Edited by Allan Bloom. Translated by James H. Nichols. Ithaca, NY: Cornell University Press, 1969.

Koktanek, Anton Mirko. *Oswald Spengler in seiner Zeit.* Munich: C. H. Beck, 1966.

von Leers, Johann. *Spenglers weltpolitisches System under der Nationalsozialistiche.* Berlin: Junker und Dünnhaupt, 1934.

Lilla, Mark. *The Shipwrecked Mind: On Political Reaction.* New York: New York Review Books, 2016.

Limbaugh, Rush. "Understanding Trump's Appeal." *Rush Limbaugh Show,* January 20, 2016. Accessed August 10, 2018. https://www.rushlimbaugh.com/daily/2016/01/20/understanding_trump_s_appeal-2/.

Linderhof, Sebastian. "Concealed Influence: Francis Parker Yockey's Plagiarism of Carl Schmitt." *Occidental Quarterly* 10, no. 4 (Winter 2010–2011): 19–62.

Lipstadt, Deborah. *Denying the Holocaust: The Growing Assault on Truth and Memory.* New York: Penguin, 1993.

Luban, Daniel. "Among the Post-liberals." *Dissent,* Winter 2020.

Maass, Sebastian. *Oswald Spengler: ein politische Biographie.* Berlin: Duncker and Humblot, 2013.

MacDonald, Kevin. "Christianity and the Ethnic Suicide of the West." *Occidental Observer,* April 27, 2015. https://www.theoccidentalobserver.net/2015/04/27/christianity-and-the-ethnic-suicide-of-the-west/.

MacDougald, Park. "The Catholic Debate over Liberalism." *City Journal,* Winter 2020.

Main, Thomas. *The Rise of the Alt-Right.* Washington, DC: Brookings Institution Press, 2018.

Mann, Thomas. "Über die Lehre Spenglers," in *Bemühungen. Neue Folge der gesammelten Abhandlungen und kleinen Aufsätze.* Berlin: S. Fischer, 1925.

Marzouki, Nadia, Olivier Roy, and Duncan McDonnell, eds. *Saving the People: How Populists Hijack Religion.* New York: Oxford University Press, 2016.

Merlio, Gilbert. *Oswald Spengler: Témoin de son temps*. Stuttgart: Akademischer Verlag Hans-Dieter Heinz, 1982.

Messer, August. *Oswald Spengler als Philosoph*. Stuttgart: Strecker and Schröder, 1924.

Michael, George. *Willis Carto and the American Far Right*. Gainesville: University of Florida Press, 2008.

Mohler, Armin. *Die konservative Revolution in Deutschland 1918–1932: Grundriss ihrer Weltanschauungen*. Stuttgart: Friedrich Vorwerk Verlag, 1950.

Moyn, Samuel. "The Alt Right's Favorite Meme Is 100 Years Old." *New York Times*, November 13, 2018.

Nolte, Ernst. *Three Faces of Fascism: Action Française, Italian Fascism, National Socialism*. Translated by Leila Vennewitz. New York: Holt, Rinehart and Winston, 1966.

Oakland Tribune. "Mystery Surrounds Man Seized with Fake Passports." June 9, 1960.

O'Meara, Michael. *New Culture, New Right: Anti-liberalism in Postmodern Europe*. Bloomington, IN: 1st Books, 2004.

Pareto, Vilfredo. *Mind and Society*. Translated by Arthur Livingston. New York: Harcourt Brace, 1935.

Pius XII. *Summi Pontificatus*. Holy See (Vatican), October 20, 1939. http://www.vatican.va/content/pius-xii/en/encyclicals/documents/hf_p-xii_enc_20101939_summi-pontificatus.html.

Potok, Mark. "To Russia with Love: Why Southern U.S. Extremists Are Mad about Vladimir Putin," *Daily Beast*, August 22, 2018. https://www.thedailybeast.com/to-russia-with-love-why-southern-us-extremists-are-mad-about-vladimir-putin.

Reno, R. R. *Return of the Strong Gods: Nationalism, Populism, and the Future of the West*. Washington, DC: Regnery Gateway, 2019.

San Francisco Examiner. "Passports Jail Mystery Visitor." June 9, 1960.

Schmitt, Carl. *The Concept of the Political*. Translated by George Schwab. Chicago: University of Chicago Press, 1996.

——. *The Crisis of Parliamentary Democracy*. Translated by Ellen Kennedy. Cambridge, MA: MIT Press, 1985.

——. *The* Nomos *of the Earth in the International Law of the* Jus Publicum Europaeum. Translated by G. L. Ulmen. Candor, NY: Telos Press, 2003.

Sheehan, Thomas. "*Diventare Dio:* Julius Evola and the Metaphysics of Fascism." In *Nietzsche in Italy*. Edited by Thomas Harrison. Palo Alto, CA: Stanford University Press, 1988.

——. "Italy: Terror on the Right." *New York Review of Books*, January 22, 1981.

Shekhovtsov, Anton. *Russia and the Western Far Right*. New York: Routledge, 2018.

Shenk, Timothy. "The Dark History of Donald Trump's Right-Wing Revolt." *Guardian*, August 16, 2016.

Sheppard, Richard. "Julius Evola, Futurism and Dada: A Case of Double Misunderstanding." In *New Studies in Dada*. Driffield, UK: Hutton Press, 1981.

Simonds, C. H. "The Strange Story of Willis Carto." *National Review,* September 10, 1971: 978–989.

Simpson, William Gayley. *Which Way Western Man?* Cooperstown, NY: Yeoman Press, 1978.

Sontheimer, Kurt. "Anti-democratic Thought in the Weimar Republic." In *The Road to Dictatorship: Germany, 1918–1933*. Edited by Theodor Eschenburg. Translated by Lawrence Wilson. London: Oswald Wolff, 1964.

Spektorowski, Alberto. "The French New Right: Multiculturalism of the Right and the Recognition/Exclusionism Syndrome." *Journal of Global Ethics* 8, no.1 (2012): 41–61.

Spencer, Richard. *The Radix Podcast. Radix Journal.* https://radixjournal.com/podcasts/.

Spengler, Oswald. *Aphorisms*. Translated by Gisela Koch-Weser O'Brien. Regnery: Chicago, 1967.

——. *The Decline of the West:* Vol. 1, *Form and Actuality.* Translated by Charles Francis Atkinson. New York: Alfred A. Knopf, 1926. Originally published as *Der Untergang des Abendlandes: Gestalt und Wirklichkeit* (Leipzig: Braumüller, 1918).

——. *The Decline of the West:* Vol. 2, *Perspectives of World History.* Translated by Charles Francis Atkinson. New York: Alfred A. Knopf, 1928. Originally published as *Der Untergang des Abendlandes: Welthistorische Perspectiven* (Munich: C. H. Beck, 1922).

——. *The Hour of Decision, Part One: Germany and World-Historical Evolution.* Translated by Charles Francis Atkinson. New York: Alfred A. Knopf, 1934. Originally published as *Jahre der Entscheidung. Deutschland und die weltgeschichtliche Entwicklung* (Munich: C. H. Beck, 1933).

——. "Is World Peace Possible?" In *Selected Essays.*

——. *Man and Technics: A Contribution to a Philosophy of Life.* Translated by Charles Francis Atkinson. New York: Alfred A. Knopf, 1932.

——. "Nietzsche and His Century." In *Selected Essays.*

——. "Pessimismus?" In *Reden und Aufsätze.* Munich: C. H. Beck, 1938.

——. "Prussianism and Socialism." In *Selected Essays.*

——. *Selected Essays.* Translated by Donald O. White. Chicago: Regnery, 1967.

——. *Spengler Letters: 1913–1936.* Translated by Arthur Phelps. London: George Allen and Unwin, 1966.

——. "Two Faces of Russia." In *Selected Essays.*

Strauss, Leo. "German Nihilism." Edited by David Janssens and Daniel Tanguay. *Interpretation* 29, no. 3 (1999): 353–379.

——. *On Tyranny.* Ithaca, NY: Cornell University Press, 1963.

Struve, Walter. *Elites Against Democracy: Leadership Ideals in Bourgeois Political Thought in Germany, 1890–1933*. Princeton, NJ: Princeton University Press, 1973.

Sunic, Tomislav. *Against Democracy and Equality: The European New Right*. New York: Peter Lang, 1990.

Taguieff, Pierre-André. "From Race to Culture: The New Right's View of European Identity." *Telos*, no. 98–99 (1993): 99–125.

——. *Sur la Nouvelle Droite: Jalons d'une analyse critique*. Paris: Descartes and Cie, 1994.

Taylor, Edmund. "Germany: Where Fascism and Communism Meet." *Reporter*, April 13, 1954: 10–16.

Toth, Czaba. "Full text of Viktor Orbán's speech at Băile Tuşnad (Tusnádfürdő) of 26 July 2014." *Budapest Beacon*, July 29, 2014. Accessed July 26, 2018. https://budapestbeacon.com/full-text-of-viktor-orbans-speech-at-baile-tusnad-tusnad furdo-of-26-july-2014/.

Warren, Donald I. "The Politics of the Displaced Majority." *Telos*, no. 95 (1993): 147–160.

——. *The Radical Center: Middle Americans and the Politics of Alienation*. Notre Dame, IN: University of Notre Dame Press, 1976.

——. "White Americans as a Minority." *Telos*, no. 104 (1995): 127–134.

Washington Post. "NYA: Alive & Well Here." December 22, 1969.

——. "Reds, Nazis Renew Act." March 31, 1954.

Watts, Edward J. *The Final Pagan Generation: Rome's Unexpected Path to Christianity*. Berkeley: University of California Press, 2015.

Weber, Max. *Essays in Sociology*. Translated by C. Wright Mills and H. H Gerth. New York: Oxford University Press, 1958.

Weigert, Hans. "Oswald Spengler, Twenty-Five Years Later." *Foreign Affairs* 21, no. 1 (1942).

Williams, Thomas Chatterton. "The French Origins of 'You Will Not Replace Us.'" *New Yorker*, November 27, 2017.

Wolin, Richard. *The Seduction of Unreason: The Intellectual Romance with Fascism from Nietzsche to Postmodernism*. Princeton, NJ: Princeton University Press, 2004.

Yockey, Francis Parker. *The Enemy of Europe*. In *The World in Flames*.

——. [Ulick Varange, pseud.]. *Imperium*. 2 vols. London: Westropa Press, 1948.

——. *The Proclamation of London*. In *The World in Flames*.

——. "What Is Behind the Hanging of the Eleven Jews in Prague?" In *The World in Flames*.

——. "The World in Flames: An Estimate of the World Situation." In *The World in Flames*.

——. *The World in Flames: The Shorter Writings of Francis Parker Yockey*. Edited by Kerry Bolton and John Morgan. N.p.: Centennial Edition Publishing, 2020.

Zeskind, Leonard. *Blood and Politics: The History of the White Nationalist Movement from the Margins to the Mainstream*. New York: Farrar, Straus and Giroux, 2009.

Zúquete, José Pedro. *The Identitarians: The Movement Against Globalism and Islam in Europe*. Notre Dame, IN: University of Notre Dame Press, 2018.

INDEX

INDEX

INDEX

INDEX